TENSE LOGIC

SYNTHESE LIBRARY

MONOGRAPHS ON EPISTEMOLOGY,

LOGIC, METHODOLOGY, PHILOSOPHY OF SCIENCE,

SOCIOLOGY OF SCIENCE AND OF KNOWLEDGE,

AND ON THE MATHEMATICAL METHODS OF

SOCIAL AND BEHAVIORAL SCIENCES

Managing Editor:

JAAKKO HINTIKKA, *Academy of Finland and Stanford University*

Editors:

ROBERT S. COHEN, *Boston University*

DONALD DAVIDSON, *Rockefeller University and Princeton University*

GABRIËL NUCHELMANS, *University of Leyden*

WESLEY C. SALMON, *University of Arizona*

VOLUME 111

ROBERT P. McARTHUR

Colby College, Waterville, Maine, U.S.A.

TENSE LOGIC

D. REIDEL PUBLISHING COMPANY

DORDRECHT-HOLLAND / BOSTON-U.S.A.

ISBN 90-277-0697-2

Published by D. Reidel Publishing Company,
P.O. Box 17, Dordrecht, Holland

Sold and distributed in the U.S.A., Canada, and Mexico
by D. Reidel Publishing Company, Inc.
Lincoln Building, 160 Old Derby Street, Hingham,
Mass. 02043, U.S.A.

PREFACE

This monograph is designed to provide an introduction to the principal areas of tense logic. Many of the developments in this ever-growing field have been intentionally excluded to fulfill this aim. Length also dictated a choice between the alternative notations of A. N. Prior and Nicholas Rescher — two pioneers of the subject. I choose Prior's because of the syntactical parallels with the language it symbolizes and its close ties with other branches of logical theory, especially modal logic.

The first chapter presents a wider view of the material than later chapters. Several lines of development are consequently not followed through the remainder of the book, most notably metric systems. Although it is important to recognize that the unadorned Prior-symbolism can be enriched in various ways it is an advanced subject as to how to actually carry off these enrichments. Readers desiring more information are referred to the appropriate literature. Specialists will notice that only the first of several quantificational versions of tense logic is proven complete in the final chapter. Again constraints of space are partly to blame. The proof for the 'star' systems is wildly complex and at the time of this writing is not yet ready for publication.

It is a pleasure to thank Professors Hugues Leblanc, Henry Kyburg, Frank Parker, Mr. Daniel Cohen, and Mr. Russell Wahl for their generous assistance and helpful comments on earlier versions of this work. I should also like to thank Colby College's Humanities Grant Committee for a research grant during the summer of 1974.

R.P.M.

TABLE OF CONTENTS

CHAPTER 1

AN OVERVIEW OF TENSE LOGIC

1.1. INTRODUCTION

As P. F. Strawson noted in his *Introduction to Logical Theory*,[1] standard logic seems ill-adapted to deal with statements containing tensed verbs or explicit temporal references. For example, we say things like 'There were women among the survivors' but the existential quantifier $\exists x$ is read 'There *is* (timelessly) an x such that', and the relation of predicate expressions to their subjects is also presumed to be timeless.[2] Hence, trying to symbolize this statement results in the awkward

(1) $(\exists x)(x$ *is* a woman & x *is* a person who was among the survivors)

where both occurrences of '*is*' are taken to be timeless. One of the consequences of this deficiency in standard logic is that arguments whose premisses and conclusion contain tensed verbs may be pronounced invalid, even though they are intuitively valid. So, in the following case

(2)   John is running

(therefore) John will have run

most would agree that the conclusion follows from the premiss, but this cannot be represented by standard logical means.

Responses to complaints such as Strawson's have fallen, until recently, into two classes. Some, such as W. V. Quine, argue that all statements containing tensed verbs can be paraphrased into an atemporal form and represented in an extended version of standard logic.[3] Others take the situation outlined above as evidence of the inherent limitation of formal logic, showing that it is incapable of representing the statements of ordinary language. This is Strawson's position.[4]

In the last few years a third response has appeared which takes the form of developing a (formal) logic of tense and temporality. Slipping between the alternatives posed by Quine and Strawson, such logics offer a neat compromise. On one hand, temporality is preserved against Quine's atemporal paraphrases. And on the other hand, the scope of formal logic is extended so as to meet, at least in this area, Strawson's misgivings about the limits of logic.

In addition to the formalization of tensed statements, the systematization of inferences involving such statements has been a primary aim of tense logicians. But here, as in all non-standard areas of logical theory, a difficult question arises as to which assumptions about tense – and, as we shall soon point out, about time – should be taken axiomatically in the development of deductive systems of tense logic. Without an exploration of various possibilities any proposed answer to this question will inevitably seem arbitrary. Thus many systems of tense logic have been created which incorporate differing tense logical principles. Such systems allow the investigation of these principles taken singly and in groups. And, in this manner, the covert assumptions behind intuitive appraisals of tensed arguments are brought to the surface.

1.2. THE FORMALITIES OF TENSED STATEMENTS

As regards temporal reference, two distinct categories of statements can be distinguished. These are:

(i) Temporally definite
(ii) Temporally indefinite.[5]

The first category includes all those statements having no temporal reference whatsoever – so-called *atemporal* statements – such as '5 is a prime number' as well as those with specific temporal references, e.g.,

(3)   It always rains in Boston.

The essential feature of temporally definite statements is that their truth-values are independent of the time of their utterance. Or, to put the matter in a somewhat different manner, such statements do not convey any positional information concerning the temporal relation of the speaker and the event or state of affairs depicted. Of course, hybrids of the sort

(4)   It *rained* in Boston on May 12, 1973

are not unusual. Although some positional information is imparted by (4), i.e., that the time of utterance is later than May 12, 1973, to convey this fact is generally not the primary intent of the speaker. In such cases, statements like (4) can be thought of as if they were expressed with atemporal verbs (e.g., It rains in Boston on May 12, 1973). When the positional information is the point of the statement, it can be parsed as a conjunction of a temporally definite statement and a temporally indefinite statement, e.g.,

(4′)   It rains in Boston on May 12, 1973 and May 12, 1973 is now past.

Since the tense of the verb, as already noted, does not play an important role in temporally definite statements, it is not surprising that tense logic is more concerned with the second category: temporally indefinite statements. Several examples of this sort of statement are:

(5)   Richmond was the capital of the Confederacy.

(6)   It is sunny and warm today.

(7)   Montreal will be the site of the next Olympic Games.

Note that the truth-value of all these is very much dependent upon the time of utterance, a property we can take as essential to this category of statement.

English has three basic tenses which may enter into the composition of a temporally indefinite statement. These are the (simple) past, present, and future tenses. Following the analogy of the formal analysis of negation in ordinary logic, it is convenient to think of statements in these three tenses as compounds consisting of a one-place statement operator – which picks up the tense – and an interior statement. Utilizing the symbol F for the future tense operator, P for the past tense operator, and T for the present tense operator, statements (5)–(7) above can be partially symbolized as follows.

(5′) P(Richmond is the capital of the Confederacy)

(6′) T(It is sunny and warm today)

(7′) F(Montreal is the site of the next Olympic Games)

Note however that construing the tense operators as statement operators requires the verb in the (temporally indefinite) interior statement to have some tense or other. Hence a certain redundancy is present in (6′); not only does the statement operator T signify present tense but the interior statement in is the present tense as well. Thus the T operator is superfluous and can be dispensed with. This leaves us with only two tense operators – F and P.

The function of F and P is to strip all but present tenseness from the main verb in the original statement and pack the tense into the prefix. Consequently, reading F as 'It will be the case that' and P as 'It has been the case that' seems appropriate. When symbols are translated back into English this results in some artificiality, e.g., 'It will be the case that it rains in Boston', but no more than arises from the formal reading of the negation operator as 'It is not the case that'.

Utilizing the two tense operators in combination allows the symbolization of other tenses as well. Below are statements in two common perfect tenses (past and future) with symbolizations.

(8)   It had rained in Boston = PPp

(9)   It will have rained in Boston = FPp

(Note that p stands for the atomic statement 'It rains in Boston'). With the addition of the truth-functional connectives & (conjunction) and $\sim$ (negation) other constructions are possible, e.g., 'It did rain in Boston but isn't now' being Pp & $\sim p$.

Negations in statements containing tense operators must be handled with care, for there is a considerable difference between

(10) $F\sim p$

and

(11) $\sim Fp$.

The best rendition of (10) (with p still doing duty for 'It rains in Boston') is

(10′)   It won't always rain in Boston

whereas (11) would be

(11′)   It will never rain in Boston.

The reasons for these paraphrases are straightforward. Fp translates 'p at sometime in the future' and, hence $F\sim p$ translates '$\sim p$ sometime in the future'. But $\sim Fp$, being the denial of Fp, translates 'p at no time in the future'. The same considerations apply, *mutatis mutandis*, to P.

The Law of Double Negation operatires as usual, as shown by the equivalences ($\equiv$ is the biconditional symbol)

(12) $\sim\sim Fp \equiv Fp$

(13) $\sim\sim Pp \equiv Pp$

(14) $F\sim\sim p \equiv Fp$

(15) $P\sim\sim p \equiv Pp$

However, $\sim F\sim p$ and Fp ($\sim P\sim p$ and Pp) are not equivalent.

As the foregoing discussion suggests, $\sim F\sim$ stands to F in a manner analogous to the relation of the universal quantifier $\forall$ to the existential quantifier $\exists$. $\sim F\sim p$ says that p is never (in the future) false — and hence is always true — and Fp says that p is true at *some* time in the future. The past tense operator P works in a similar fashion. It is convenient to have special symbols for $\sim F\sim$ and $\sim P\sim$ due to their frequent use. Hence we shall adopt G ('It will *always* be the case that') as shorthand for $\sim F\sim$, and H ('It has *always* been the case that') as shorthand for $\sim P\sim$. These two additional operators permit a simple capturing of the *omnitemporal assertion* of a statement p — i.e., the truth of p at all times: past, present, and future — by means of the conjunction Hp & $(p$ & $Gp)$.

Further sophistication of the formal machinery developed thus far is possible. One way to extend the applicability of the tense operators is to provide them with metric indices. These, written as superscripts, permit the reference to specific temporal intervals in the past or future of the time of utterance. For example, suppose we want a symbolism for 'It will rain one hour from now' which is more precise than the bald Fp. Understanding an hour to be the basic time interval (for the sake of the example), this statement could be written F^1p, i.e., 'It will be the case that one interval hence it rains'. Using the metric variables m and n, where it is presumed that $n > m$, this style of tense formulation permits a sharpness not previously available in our rendition of the future perfect tense. Whereas we had FPp before, now 'It will have been the case that p' can be written $F^n P^m p$.[6]

Within the confines of a metric tense logic which disallows free variables of any sort, all of the non-metric operators may be defined by means of metric quantification. These definitions are as follows.

(16) $Fp =_{\text{df}} (\exists n)F^n p$

(17) $Pp =_{\text{df}} (\exists n)P^n p$

(18) $Gp =_{\text{df}} (\forall n)F^n p$

(19) $Hp =_{\text{df}} (\forall n)P^n p$

But as the reader may have noticed, the range of the metric variables must be carefully specified. For example, if zero is a possible value of n, then $(\exists n)F^n p$ will translate 'p is now or will (sometime) be the case' insofar as $F^0 p$

is equivalent to simply p. On the other hand, if negative integers are also permitted, then $(\exists n)F^n p$ fails to indicate futurity at all. $F^{-n}p$ is equivalent to $P^n p$, so $(\exists n)F^n p$, with n ranging over all the integers (positive and negative) is 'p is the case at some time'. If two runs of variables were utilized, then a certain economy could be acheived in the stock of primitive symbols. For in such a case, P could be introduced by definition from F by means of negative metric indices. As a final point, note that even when the indices are understood as positive integers, $F^n P^n p$ is equivalent to p.

Intermediate between the unadorned P–F–G–H system and the full metricization of the operators are notations which utilize an operator for the temporal adverb 'now'. Instead of permitting reference to many temporal intervals like metric notations, such systems permit reference to one interval, *viz.* the present. Consider the two statements:

(20)   I learned there would be an earthquake.

(21)   I learned there would now be an earthquake.

In the first of these the earthquake-event could have occurred several days ago, or could occur today or during the next few days. But in the second the event is explicitly stated to take place today. Without 'now' actually being said a similar difference crops up between the following statements.

(22)   It was then true that there would be an earthquake.

(23)   It was then true that there will be an earthquake.

In (22) the earthquake can be past, present, or future whereas in (23) it must be in the future.

To capture these references to the present by means of the adverb 'now' (or an equivalent device) a symbolism is required to have an 'adverbial' operator. Let N be such an operator. Statements (22) and (23) can then be put into symbols as follows (p stands for 'There is an earthquake').

(22′)   *PFp*

(23′)   *PNFp*

Note that the placement of the N in (23′) is significant. *PFNp* would translate 'It was true that there would now be an earthquake'.

The operator N is superfluous when simply prefixed to a statement, as was earlier noted about the 'present tense' operator T (p. 3). Hence the equivalences

(24) $Np \equiv p$

(25) $NFp \equiv Fp$

surely hold. But N is non-superfluous when it occurs within the scope of tense operators, as in (23').[7]

Additional expressive power is provided by introducing modal statement operators into a tense logic. The two we shall be concerned with are M (possibility) and L (necessity). Their introduction can be accomplished in two ways. Either the modal operators can be defined in terms of the tense operators, and, hence, added to the defined signs of the system, or they can be given a separate role and introduced as extra primitive operators. Having the modal operators available permits the symbolization of many statements which combine tensed verbs and modalites, e.g.,

(26)   It is possible that Jones will win the race.

(27)   If gunpowder is ignited an explosion will necessarily result.

(28)   Ceasar had to cross the Rubicon.

Statements (26)–(28) are symbolized with both modal and tense operators as follows.

(26') MF(Jones wins the race)

(27')   (Gunpowder is ignited) $\supset FL$(An explosion results)

(28') PL(Ceasar crosses the Rubicon)

1.3. INTERPRETING TENSED STATEMENTS. I

The development of an adequate semantic interpretation of the tense operators requires that the informal explication of F and P previously given be made more rigorous. Following accepted practice, we shall devise semantic models for tense logic which can be used to specify the definitions of tense logical truth, validity, entailment, satisfaction, and so forth. We shall also have to insure a strong conceptual basis for any such semantics in order that it have applicability to the ordinary usage of tensed statements.

In standard logic without quantifiers the primary semantic vehicle is the truth-value assignment. Often represented, in part, by a line of a truth table, such an assignment is a pairing of a truth-value – here, 1 ('true') or 0 ('false') – with every atomic statement. To be more precise, a truth-value assignment is thus a function from the set of atomic statements to $\{1, 0\}$. As is well known, any truth-functional compound has a determinate truth-value on every truth-value assignment which may be calculated by means of the familiar rules for the various connectives.

Furthermore, a set of statements can be generated out of any truth-value assignment; *viz.* the set of all statements true on the assignment. Two features of such sets should be noted at this point. First, every statement or its negation is sure to be a member of one of these sets; and, second, these sets are sure to be consistent. If each member of one of these sets records some fact, then the entire set may be thought of as a *world state*, or as a *possible world*.[8] The members of the set describe the way the world is or how it might be. Of course, in standard logic, since no temporal distinctions are recognized, these world states are atemporal. They are often thought of as depicting all events as spread out in four dimensions – time being just one of them. However they ultimately are understood, we prefer to think of the truth-value assignment instead of the corresponding set of statements as a world state.[9]

In tense logic, a truth-value assignment can conveniently be understood as representing a *temporal* state of the world. It gives an accounting of the contents of an interval of time, or, alternatively, what is happening at a certain date, by means of the assignment of truth-values to atomic statements.

The truth-values of statements not containing tense operators are handled as usual, but the truth-values of tense logically compound statements – for example, those of the sort *FA* – cannot be calculated solely on the basis of a *single* truth-value assignment, since they explicitly relate two (or more) temporal intervals. Thus having agreed with Wittgenstein that 'The world is all that is the case',[10] at least at a given temporal interval, it is reasonable to think of a depiction of the passage of time as requiring a series of these temporal world-states. Such a series can be formally protrayed as a *sequence* of truth-value assignments; one for each temporal world-state in the series. And, like any sequence, it can be generated out of a set (here of truth-value assignments) by imposing an ordering relation on its membership.

We can take our cue from ordinary thinking about time, which recognizes the dyadic relation of earlier and later. Notice that this relation is commonly held to have definite properties. Few would dispute that the earlier/later relation is *transitive* (if x is earlier than y, and y is earlier than z, then x is earlier than z), *irreflexive* (no x is earlier than itself), and *asymmetrical* (if x is earlier than y, then y cannot be earlier than x).

We want to employ an analogue of the earlier/later relation, but we require it to be a relation on temporal world-states, and not on the more abstract temporal intervals. For we have no means (in general) of specifying a temporal interval apart from those events and states of affairs which take place during the interval, i.e., what we have been calling a world state. This is a rather Leibnizian conception of time as derivative rather than a Newtonian conception of the series of temporal intervals (independent of the world-states) as absolute and primary. Considering the *relata* as temporal world-states has the added advantage of allowing us to talk of the *past* as what has taken place and of the future as what *will* take place (or what may take place).

Returning to our modeling of the temporal series, one technical problem arises which fortunately has an easy solution. If we simply impose a dyadic relation on a set of truth-value assignments in order to effect a succession, we preclude the possibility of the same assignment occurring twice (or more) in the series. Hence, under our present view, this eliminates the possibility of the world being the same on two different occasions. Not allowing an assignment to crop up twice makes it a *logical* truth that the world does not repeat, which hardly seems likely.

Hence, to skirt this difficulty, we pair each truth-value assignment with an index (some real number) and allow the same assignment, albeit with a different index, to be used more than once. Thus we end up with a set − to be denoted by Ω − of pairs of the sort $\langle \varphi, i \rangle$, where φ is a truth-value assignment and i is its index. The same assignment, to repeat, can turn up in two or more pairs, e.g., in $\langle \varphi, i \rangle$ and $\langle \varphi, j \rangle$, so long as their indices differ (i.e., $i \neq j$). The dyadic relation which orders the members of Ω we shall refer to as R. Our concern will be exclusively with the truth-value assignments, rather than the indices, in the members of Ω, so we shall henceforth speak of the members of Ω as $\varphi, \mu, \varphi', \mu'$, etc., instead of the more cumbersome $\langle \varphi, i \rangle, \langle \mu, j \rangle$, etc. So, φ, μ, and so on, will be presumed to be *indexed* truth-value assignments.

The pair $\langle \Omega, R \rangle$, then, for us represents a temporal succession of world states. As such, $\langle \Omega, R \rangle$ may be thought of as a chronicle or *history*, recording events as they take place at various (ordered) temporal intervals. Of course, this stretches the ordinary sense of the term *history* somewhat. First of all, we are accustomed to thinking in terms of one history − The History − and not of possible histories. Second, the earlier/later relation (represented by R) is normally considered as having specific properties as mentioned above, and we will permit R here to have *any* combination of properties. In fact, the consequences of varying the properties of R will be a central part of our study of tense logic.

We set out to find a way to formally interpret tense logically compound statements and we are now near that goal. To serve a role similar to that of unadorned truth-value assignments in standard logic, we shall make use of *historical moments.* [11] These shall be triples of the sort $\langle \Omega, R, \varphi \rangle$ where Ω is a set of indexed truth-value assignments, R is a dyadic relation on Ω, and φ is a member of Ω. φ serves as the representative of some temporal world-state, and its past and future are given by R and Ω. Hence, if $R(\varphi, \mu)$ (i.e., φ bears R to μ), then the historical moment $\langle \Omega, R, \mu \rangle$ is part of φ's future, and if $R(\mu, \varphi)$, then the historical moment $\langle \Omega, R, \mu \rangle$ is part of φ's past. Of course, there may be no member μ of Ω such that $R(\varphi, \mu)$. If so, then φ has no future; it is, one might say, the last moment of time. Similarly, there may be no member μ of Ω such that $R(\mu, \varphi)$, making φ the first moment of time. Actually, in strict terms φ and μ are not moments at all, only the triples $\langle \Omega, R, \varphi \rangle$ and $\langle \Omega, R, \mu \rangle$ count as historical moments. If this seems overly fussy, the reader should note that $\langle \Omega, R', \varphi \rangle$ is an historical moment quite different from $\langle \Omega, R, \varphi \rangle$ insofar as R' is a different relation than R. This fact should be kept in mind, because we shall soon be speaking of *all* historical moments and shall mean any triple $\langle \Omega, R, \varphi \rangle$ no matter what the make-up of Ω, R, and φ.

The interpretation of atomic and truth-functionally compound statements at historical moments follows the lines of standard logic. The various tense logically compound statements are interpreted as follows, with A as a syntactical variable for any statement whatever.

(i) FA is true at $\langle \Omega, R, \varphi \rangle$ if A is true at *some* $\langle \Omega, R, \mu \rangle$ such that $R(\varphi, \mu)$

(ii) PA is true at $\langle \Omega, R, \varphi \rangle$ if A is true at *some* $\langle \Omega, R, \mu \rangle$ such that $R(\mu, \varphi)$

(iii) GA is true at $\langle \Omega, R, \varphi \rangle$ if A is true at *every* $\langle \Omega, R, \mu \rangle$ such that $R(\varphi, \mu)$

(iv) HA is true at $\langle \Omega, R, \varphi \rangle$ if A is true at *every* $\langle \Omega, R, \mu \rangle$ such that $R(\mu, \varphi)$

Note these truth conditions for the tense operators do preserve the definitional equivalences of GA and $\sim F \sim A$, and HA and $\sim P \sim A$. By way of illustration, suppose φ is a member of Ω and A is true at every $\langle \Omega, R, \mu \rangle$ such that $R(\varphi, \mu)$. Then $\sim A$ is false at every $\langle \Omega, R, \mu \rangle$ such that $R(\varphi, \mu)$, hence $F\sim A$ is false and $\sim F\sim A$ is true at $\langle \Omega, R, \varphi \rangle$. The case for HA and PA is similar.

When added to the usual truth conditions from standard logic, the truth conditions given above for the tense operators provide adequate definitions of truth and falsity for the whole of tense logic. In turn the other semantical concepts – satisfiability, validity, and entailment – are easily defined as well. A set of statements is satisfiable in a tense logic if there is a historical moment of that logic at which all the members of the set are true. A statement is valid if it is true at every historical moment of the logic. Finally, a set S entails a statement A if $S \cup \{\sim A\}$ is not satisfiable.

It is easily verified that all valid (tautological, as some say) statements of standard, truth-functional logic are valid in any tense logic given the foregoing definitions. The argument is quite straightforward and runs as follows: Suppose A is a valid statement of truth-functional logic. Then A is sure to be true on every truth-value assignment. Hence, since historical moments are truth-value assignments embedded in histories, which in turn are sequences of truth-value assignments, A is true at every historical moment. Thus A is valid given the definition of validity above. This result is a bit stronger than it may, at first, appear. For not only are valid statements from truth-functional logic valid here, but all valid *schemata* are as well. Consequently, (tensed) statements such as $Fp \supset (q \supset Fp)$, $Fp \vee \sim Fp$, and so forth, are validated by the same argument.

By varying the specified properties of the relation R, histories and historical moments provide semantical interpretations for a variety of tense logic systems.

Furthermore, tense logics can be arranged in a series and generated by placing increasingly stringent restrictions on R. A *minimal* system, called K_t in the literature, thus arises in whose histories R may be any relation whatever. Then by requiring R to be transitive, connected,[12] non-ending and non-beginning, dense, symmetrical, etc., other systems which are extensions of K_t can be semantically constructed. Thus system building in tense logic can proceed either syntactically, by taking a group of statements as axioms, or semantically, by making certain assumptions about the properties of temporal succession, i.e. the properties of R.

Since many tense logics were first investigated from the semantical perspective, they are often thought of in semantical terms. For example, systems requiring R to be transitive in historical moments as well as connected are called *linear* tense logics, those in which R is transitive but unconnected are called *branching* tense logics, and systems in which R is transitive, reflexive, and symmetrical are called *circular* tense logics. Here, once more, the point of taking the relation R to relate temporal world states and not temporal intervals. For it would make little sense to speak of *time* as branching or circular, although it is at least coherent to say that temporal world states can be arranged in a branching, etc., order.

1.4. INTERPRETING TENSED STATEMENTS. II

We opened this chapter by noting Strawson's discomfort over the way tensed quantificational statements are handled in standard logic. In this section we shall extend the semantics introduced in the previous section to quantifiers.

Recent work in quantificational logic has resulted in a *substitutional interpretation of the quantifiers*. Here domains, domain interpretations, and so forth are eschewed in favor of the same truth-value assignments one finds in non-quantificational logics. A (universal) quantification of the sort $(\forall X)A$ is counted as true on a truth-value assignment so long as all of its substitution instances are true on the assignment, and a (existential) quantification of the sort $(\exists X)A$ is counted as true if some of its substitution instances are true.[13] Thus statements involving quantifiers can easily be interpreted by means of the histories and historical moments already deployed.

In order for the substitutional semantics to conveniently pan out we shall insist that our quantificational logics are equipped with two runs of individual symbols. We shall call variables that may be bound by quantifiers *individual variables*, and those which occur unbound we shall call *individual constants*. X and Y will be used to represent individual variables and C will be used for individual constants. An *atomic statement* of a quantificational tense logic is taken to be any statement of the sort $\mathbf{F}^m(C_1, C_2, \ldots, C_m)$, where $\mathbf{F}^m$ is an m-place predicate and $C_1, C_2, \ldots, C_m$ are individual constants. Truth-value assignments are defined as before, i.e., as functions from the set of atomic statements to $\{1, 0\}$.

Hence using $A(C/X)$ to indicate the result of replacing (the individual variable) X by (the individual constant) C everywhere in A, truth conditions for quantificational statements can be given as follows:

(i) $(\forall X)A$ is true at $\langle \Omega, R, \varphi \rangle$ if $A(C/X)$ is true for every individual constant C

(ii) $(\exists X)A$ is true at $\langle \Omega, R, \varphi \rangle$ if $A(C/X)$ is true for at least one individual constant C

To illustrate the matter, suppose 'Everything will cease to exist', i.e., $(\forall x)Ff(x)$ ($f(x)$: 'x ceases to exist') is true at $\langle \Omega, R, \varphi \rangle$. Then by the truth conditions above, $Ff(a_1)$, $Ff(a_2)$, $Ff(a_3)$, etc., must be true, where a_1, a_2, a_3, etc., are the individual constants. But according to the truth condition for statements of the sort FA, for each of these there must be an historical moment at which it is true. However, no two need be true at the same historical moment, there could even be a unique historical moment for each. Or, on the other hand, all could be true at the same historical moment.

Our semantics for quantificational tense logic justifies understanding many predicates as tensed. Thus when r means 'is in the room', the atomic statement $r(a_1)$ is taken as asserting that a_1 is *now* in the room. On the other hand, $n(a_2)$ – translating 'a_2 is a prime number' – is probably best regarded as an atemporal statement rather than as asserting that a_2 is *now* a prime number. So far, however, we have not built into our quantifiers a similar latitude. They range over all individual constants at all times (i.e., historical moments). It would be more in keeping with our goal of providing reasonable formalizations of tensed discourse if the quantifiers were interpreted as ranging over only that part of the class of all individual constants which is relevant to the historical moment at which the quantification is being evaluated. To effect this changed understanding of the quantifiers requires a *free* quantification theory.[14]

For our purposes, free quantificational logics permit individual constants to be non-designating at some historical moments. It cannot be presumed, therefore, that any given individual constant automatically counts as a legitimate substitution for a bound variable of quantification. For example, suppose the statement 'The first woman president will be elected in the year 2020' is true (now). With a_1 standing for 'the first first woman president' and e standing for 'is elected in the year 2020', this would be symbolized $Fe(a_1)$. By the usual laws of quantification, we are entitled to infer from this that $(\exists x)Fe(x)$ is true, i.e., 'There is an x such that it will be elected in the year 2020'. But suppose the person who will be elected in 2020 has not yet been born. Then $(\exists x)Fe(x)$ is false, if $\exists x$ is taken to mean 'There *now* is an x such that', which seems appropriate. Hence the inference must be blocked, and this amounts to laying on the restriction that not every individual constant may be legitimately substituted for bound variables. Obviously we need to change the truth conditions given earlier for the quantifiers so that they no longer range over all individual constants.

To effect this freeing of the quantifiers from ranging over all the individual constants in all of the historical moments, we introduce the simple expedient of pairing each truth-value assignment with a (possibly empty) set of individual constants. This set can intuitively be thought of as the set of all terms which designate at that moment. So the elements of Ω are now *pairs* of the sort $\langle \varphi, E \rangle$, where φ is as before (an indexed truth-value assignment) and E is a set of individual constants, and historical moments are of the sort $\langle \Omega, R, \langle \varphi, E \rangle \rangle$.

This change calls for revised truth conditions for the two quantifiers.

(i) $(\forall X)A$ is true at $\langle \Omega, R, \langle \varphi, E \rangle \rangle$ if $A(C/X)$ is true *for every C in E*

(ii) $(\exists X)A$ is true at $\langle \Omega, R, \langle \varphi, E \rangle \rangle$ if $A(C/X)$ is true *for at least one C in E.*

Note, however, that each statement still has a truth-value at every historical moment. It is also possible to relax this requirement and further alter the quantificational semantics. We can *relativize* each truth-value assignment to a set E, and only assign values to atomic statements whose individual constants (if any) are members of E. This will leave the other atomic statements *unvalued* (i.e., without a truth-value) on this truth-value assignment, and this will carry over to many compound statements as well. Since the precise formalization of this semantics is rather complex, we shall leave the details for Chapter 5.

Either of the free interpretations of the quantifiers we have mentioned meets, in a rather adequate manner, Strawson's complaints about tenses and formal logics. For both $\forall$ and $\exists$ are fully temporal and can be read 'For every x now ...' and 'For at least one x now ...', respectively. Returning to the issue of the symbolization of 'There were women among the survivors', we can now put it as follows ($w(x)$: 'x is a woman'; $s(x)$: 'x is among the survivors'):

(23) $P(\exists x)(w(x) \& s(x))$.

NOTES

[1] See Strawson, 1952, pp. 150–151.

[2] We shall follow the practice throughout this work of not enclosing symbols within inverted commas.

[3] The most complete discussion of this view is given in Quine, 1960. For a direct reply to Strawson, 1952, *loc. cit.*, consult Quine 1953.

[4] Strawson 1952, *loc. cit.* and *passim.*

[5] These categories are Rescher's. A full treatment of them is given in Rescher and Urquhart, 1971, Chapter III. On the same point, cf. Braude, 1973, from whom some of the details of this paragraph and the next have been borrowed.

[6] The reader interested in metric tense logics should consult Prior, 1967, Chapter 6.

[7] The material in the last three paragraphs derives from Kamp, 1971.

[8] The original user of the phrase 'possible world' in this sense was Wittgenstein. See Wittgenstein, 1961, pars. 1, 4.3, and *passim.*

[9] Quine is fond of the four dimensional view of events but not of possible worlds. Others, such as Kripke, 1963, have produced detailed accounts of atemporal possible worlds. Also see Hintikka, 1969.

[10] Wittgenstein, par. 1, reads 'The world is all that is the case'.

[11] The terms *history* and *historical moment* are Cocchiarella's. Semantics such as ours which are developed in terms of histories and historical moments are based on those introduced by Cocchiarella in 1966.

[12] A relation is connected over a set S if, for any two elements x and y of S, either $R(x, y)$ or $R(y, x)$.

[13] A complete survey of this sort of semantic theory is given in Leblanc, 1976.

[14] The two papers which launched this understanding of the quantifiers are Leblanc and Hailperin, 1959 and Hintikka, 1959.

LINEAR TENSE LOGICS

2.1. THE MINIMAL SYSTEM K_t

The minimal or basic system of tense logic is K_t, so named by E. J. Lemmon.[1] Since all of the other tense logics we discuss are extensions of K_t, we shall treat it in rather more detail than will henceforth be customary.

The primitive signs of K_t are the following:

(i) the *statement letters*: p, q, r, p', q', etc.,

(ii) the *connectives*: $\sim$ (negation) and $\supset$ (conditional),

(iii) the *tense operators*: F (future tense operator) and P (past tense operator), and

(iv) left and right parentheses as *punctuations*.

By a formula of K_t we understand any (finite) concatenation of primitive signs of K_t. Where A, B, and C are formulas, we shall take a statement of K_t to be any statement letter or any formula of the following four sorts:

(i) $\sim A$, where A is a statement,

(ii) $(A \supset B)$, where both A and B are statements,

(iii) FA, where A is a statement, and

(iv) PA, where A is a statement.

From now on, the letters A, B, and C shall stand only for statements and all outer parentheses shall be dropped.

Several other signs shall be employed in our discussion of K_t which are defined in terms of those already introduced, i.e.,

$$A \mathbin{\&} B =_{df} \sim(A \supset \sim B)$$

$$A \vee B =_{df} \sim A \supset B$$

$$A \equiv B =_{df} \sim((A \supset B) \mathbin{\&} \sim(B \supset A))$$

$$GA =_{df} \sim F \sim A$$

$$HA =_{df} \sim P \sim A$$

Finally, by the mirror image of a statement A – denoted by $MI(A)$ – we mean the result of simultaneously replacing each occurrence of F in A by P

and each occurrence of P in A by F. Thus GPA (= $\sim\overline{F}\sim PA$) is the mirror image of HFA (= $\sim P\sim FA$), $F(PA \ \& \ B)$ is the mirror image of $P(FA \ \& \ B)$, and so forth. Clearly, $MI(MI(A))$ (the mirror image of the mirror image of A) is A, and, if there are no occurrences of tense operators in A, $MI(A)$ is, again, just A.

Turning then to the deductive presentation of K_t, the reader should note that axiom schemata instead of axioms are utilized, thus allowing us to dispense with all substitution conventions.

We shall count as axioms of K_t all statements of the following seven sorts:

A1. A, where A is a tautology,

A2. $G(A \supset B) \supset (GA \supset GB)$,

A3. $H(A \supset B) \supset (HA \supset HB)$,

A4. $A \supset HFA$,

A5. $A \supset GPA$,

A6. GA, if A is an axiom, and

A7. HA, if A is an axiom.[2]

In addition, K_t has the following as its rule of inference:

RMP.   If A and $A \supset B$, then B.

By a proof in K_t of a statement A from a (possibly empty) set S of statements we understand any column of the sort

B_1

B_2

$\vdots$ $(n \geqslant 1)$

B_n

closing with A (= B_n), such that each B_i ($1 \leqslant i \leqslant n$) is either a member of S, an axiom of K_t, or follows from two previous entries, say B_e and B_f (= $B_e \supset B_i$), by RMP. We shall denote by $S \vdash A$ the provability of A from S, and, in the special case where $\emptyset \vdash A$ ($\emptyset$ denotes the empty set), we shall say that A is a theorem of K_t. If $S \vdash \sim(p \supset p)$,[3] S will be said to be inconsistent in K_t, and S will otherwise be said to be consistent.

Our primary interest in this chapter and those which follow will be in the theorems and (later) valid statements of the various systems of tense logic. So as to build into our account as much generality as possible, we will often deal with statement schemata instead of statements. Hence, when we prove that $G(A \supset B) \supset (FA \supset FB)$ is a theorem of K_t, this will be tantamount to proving the theoremhood of an infinite number of statements – the substitution instances of this schema. E.g., all of $G(p \supset q) \supset (Fp \supset Fq)$; $G((p \supset q) \supset (r \supset p')) \supset (F(p \supset q) \supset F(r \supset p'))$; and $G(Hp \supset Hq) \supset (FHp \supset FHq)$ count as theorems of K_t because they are instances of the schema $G(A \supset B) \supset (FA \supset FB)$. With this distinction in mind, we will adopt the convention of calling schemata like $G(A \supset B) \supset (FA \supset FB)$ statements, or theorems, or valid statements, or, when appropriate, axioms, when strictly they are statement schemata, theorem schemata, valid statement schemata, or axiom schemata.

Five additional rules of inference will make for shorter proofs, and have some interest of their own, so we present them with proofs as derived rules in the Meta-theorems below. Their proofs will depend upon three facts concerning provability in K_t, which carry over from standard logic.

($\vdash$ 1)   If $S \vdash A$, then, for any set S', $S \cup S' \vdash A$.

($\vdash$ 2)   If A belongs to S or is an axiom of K_t, then $S \vdash A$.

($\vdash$ 3)   If $S \vdash A$ and $S \vdash A \supset B$, then $S \vdash B$.[4]

MT1.   If $\vdash A$, then $\vdash GA$. (RG)

Proof: Suppose the column consisting of $B_1, B_2, \ldots, B_k \ (= A)$ counts as a proof of A in K_t. Then by mathematical induction on i, for each i from 1 through k, it is easily shown that $\vdash GB_i$, and, in particular, that $\vdash GB_k$ $(= \vdash GA)$. *Base Case*: By the definition of a proof, B_1 is sure to be an axiom of K_t. Hence, by A6, GB_1 is also an axiom of K_t. Thus (by ($\vdash$ 2)) $\vdash GB_1$.

Inductive Case: Suppose, for each $h < i$, that $\vdash GB_h$. Then let B_i be an axiom of K_t. By the reasoning above, it follows that $\vdash GB_i$. On the other hand, let B_i follow from two previous entries by RMP and let these entries be B_c and $B_d \ (= B_c \supset B_i)$. By the hypothesis of the induction, $\vdash GB_c$ and $\vdash GB_d$ $(= \vdash G(B_c \supset B_i))$. As concerns the latter, by A2, ($\vdash$ 2), and ($\vdash$ 3), $\vdash GB_c \supset GB_i$. Hence, by ($\vdash$ 3) again, $\vdash GB_i$.

MT2.   If $\vdash A$, then $\vdash HA$. (RH)

Proof: Proof of MT2 is similar to that of MT1, with H for G, A3 for A2, and so forth.

MT3.   If $\vdash A \supset B$, then $\vdash GA \supset GB$. (RG⊃)

Proof: Suppose $\vdash A \supset B$. Then by RG, $\vdash G(A \supset B)$. By A2, ($\vdash 2$), and ($\vdash 3$), $\vdash GA \supset GB$.

MT4.   If $\vdash A \supset B$, then $\vdash HA \supset HB$. (RH⊃)

Proof: Proof of MT4 is similar to that of MT3, with A3 for A2, and so forth.

MT5.   If $\vdash A$, then $\vdash MI(A)$. (RMI)

Proof: Suppose that $B_1, B_2, \ldots, B_k \ (= A)$ counts as a proof of A in K_t. Then by mathematical induction on i, for each i from 1 through k, it is easily shown that $\vdash MI(B_i)$, and, in particular, that $\vdash MI(B_k) \ (= \vdash MI(A))$. *Base Case*: By the definition of a proof, B_1 is sure to be an axiom of K_t. Hence so is $MI(B_1)$, since all the mirror images of A1−A7 are included in the list of axioms. Thus, $\vdash MI(B_1)$.

Inductive Case: Suppose, for each $h < i$, that $\vdash MI(B_h)$. Then let B_i be an axiom of K_t. By the reasoning above, $\vdash MI(B_i)$. On the other hand, suppose B_i follows from two previous entries by RMP, and that these entries are B_c and $B_d \ (= B_c \supset B_i)$. Then by the hypothesis of the induction, $\vdash MI(B_c)$ and $\vdash MI(B_c \supset B_i)$. But $MI(B_c \supset B_i)$ is just $MI(B_c) \supset MI(B_i)$. Hence, by ($\vdash 3$) $\vdash MI(B_i)$.

To make the proofs of the theorems of K_t (and those of the other systems as well) less tedious and easier to follow we shall adopt the convention of collapsing several moves into a single line. Under the egis of A1, we shall make use of a number of tautologies from the Statement Calculus which are listed, with identifying numbers (e.g. SC1 $= (A \supset B) \supset (\sim B \supset \sim A)$), in Appendix I. We also will make use of theorems which have already been proven and the rule of substitution of equivalents:

REQ.   If B results from the substitution of N for one or more occurrences of M in A, and if $\vdash M \equiv N$, then $\vdash B$ if $\vdash A$.

The theorems of K_t are as follows.

T1. $G(A \supset B) \supset (FA \supset FB)$

Proof:

1. $(A \supset B) \supset (\sim B \supset \sim A)$	SC1
2. $G(A \supset B) \supset G(\sim B \supset \sim A)$	RG (1)
3. $G(A \supset B) \supset (G\sim B \supset G\sim A)$	A2, SC2, RMP (2)
4. $G(A \supset B) \supset (\sim G\sim A \supset \sim G\sim B)$	SC1, SC2, RMP (3)
5. $G(A \supset B) \supset (FA \supset FB)$	Def. F/G (4)

T2.　　$H(A \supset B) \supset (PA \supset PB)$

Proof: By T1 and RMI.

T3.　　$(GA \vee GB) \supset G(A \vee B)$

Proof:

1. $A \supset (A \vee B)$	SC3
2. $B \supset (A \vee B)$	SC4
3. $GA \supset G(A \vee B)$	RG (1)
4. $GB \supset G(A \vee B)$	RG (2)
5. $(GA \vee GB) \supset G(A \vee B)$	SC5, RMP (3, 4)

T4.　　$(HA \vee HB) \supset H(A \vee B)$

Proof: By T3 and RMI.

T5.　　$F(A \& B) \supset (FA \& FB)$

Proof:

1. $(G\sim A \vee G\sim B) \supset G(\sim A \vee \sim B)$	T3
2. $\sim G(\sim A \vee \sim B) \supset \sim (G\sim A \vee G\sim B)$	SC1, RMP (1)
3. $F\sim(\sim A \vee \sim B) \supset \sim (\sim FA \vee \sim FB)$	Def. F/G (2)
4. $F(A \& B) \supset (FA \& FB)$	SC6, REQ, RMP (3)

T6.　　$P(A \& B) \supset (PA \& PB)$

Proof: By T5 and RMI.

T7.　　$G(A \& B) \equiv (GA \& GB)$

Proof:

1. $(A \& B) \supset A$	SC7
2. $(A \& B) \supset B$	SC8
3. $G(A \& B) \supset GA$	RG (1)
4. $G(A \& B) \supset GB$	RG (2)

5. $G(A \& B) \supset (GA \& GB)$ SC9, RMP $(3, 4)$
6. $A \supset (B \supset (A \& B))$ SC10
7. $GA \supset (GB \supset G(A \& B))$ RG, A2, RMP (6)
8. $(GA \& GB) \supset G(A \& B)$ SC11, RMP (7)
9. $G(A \& B) \equiv (GA \& GB)$ SC12, RMP $(5, 8)$

T8. $H(A \& B) \equiv (HA \& HB)$

Proof: By T7 and RMI.

T9. $F(A \lor B) \equiv (FA \lor FB)$

Proof:
1. $G(\sim A \& \sim B) \equiv (G\sim A \& G\sim B)$ T7
2. $\sim F\sim(\sim A \& \sim B) \equiv (\sim FA \& \sim FB)$ Def. F/G (1)
3. $\sim F(A \lor B) \equiv \sim(FA \lor FB)$ SC13, REQ (2)
4. $F(A \lor B) \equiv (FA \lor FB)$ SC14, RMP (3)

T10. $P(A \lor B) \equiv (PA \lor PB)$

Proof: By T9 and RMI.

T11. $PGA \supset A$

Proof:
1. $\sim A \supset HF\sim A$ A3
2. $\sim HF\sim A \supset \sim\sim A$ SC1, RMP (1)
3. $P\sim F\sim A \supset \sim\sim A$ Def. P/H (2)
4. $PGA \supset \sim\sim A$ Def. F/G (3)
5. $PGA \supset A$ SC15, REQ (4)

T12. $FHA \supset A$

Proof: By T11 and RMI.

Truth and the other semantic notions are defined in K_t in terms of historical moments. These, as discussed in Chapter 1, are triples of the sort $\langle \Omega, R, \varphi \rangle$, where Ω is a set of (indexed) truth-value assignments (i.e. functions from the set of statement letters to $\{1, 0\}$), R is *any* relation on the membership of Ω, and φ is a member of Ω.

A statement A, then, is true at an historical moment $\langle \Omega, R, \varphi \rangle$ if:

(1) A is a statement letter, $\varphi(A) = 1$,[5]

(2) A is of the sort $\sim B, B$ is not true at $\langle\Omega, R, \varphi\rangle$,

(3) A is of the sort $B \supset C$, either B is not true at $\langle\Omega, R, \varphi\rangle$ or C is,

(4) A is of the sort FB, B is true at some $\langle\Omega, R, \mu\rangle$ such that $R(\varphi, \mu)$, and

(5) A is of the sort PB, B is true at some $\langle\Omega, R, \mu\rangle$ such that $R(\mu, \varphi)$.

(Note that the truth conditions for the defined connectives and tense operators are easily formulated given the above five clauses).

Although it is not essential to do so, we will assume that Ω is the set of *all* of the indexed truth-value assignments and hence is invariant in the historical moments of K_t.[6] Consequently, historical moments differ only in the makeup of R or in the specific member of Ω which appears as the third term. When a statement A comes out true at every historical moment containing the relation R, we shall say that A is *R-valid* in K_t. And a statement A is *valid* in K_t, if it is R-valid for *every* relation R.

A set S of statements is satisfiable in K_t if there is an historical moment of K_t at which all of the members of S are (simultaneously) true. Finally, if a set S and a statement A are such that $S \cup \{\sim A\}$ is not satisfiable in K_t, S will be said to *entail A* in K_t.

Although we will put off to a later chapter a discussion of the metatheory of this semantics for K_t, it may be helpful to the reader to run through several semantic proofs of validity for axioms and theorems of K_t.

(1) $G(A \supset B) \supset (GA \supset GB)$ (A2)

Suppose $G(A \supset B)$ is true at some historical moment of K_t, say $\langle\Omega, R, \varphi\rangle$, and that $GA \supset GB$ is not true at $\langle\Omega, R, \varphi\rangle$. Then GA is true at $\langle\Omega, R, \varphi\rangle$ and GB is false. Hence at every historical moment $\langle\Omega, R, \mu\rangle$ such that $R(\varphi, \mu)$, both $A \supset B$ and A are true. Hence B is true as well. But this contradicts the initial assumption of the falsity of $GA \supset GB$ at $\langle\Omega, R, \varphi\rangle$. Hence, by reductio ad absudum, if $G(A \supset B)$ is true at an historical moment of K_t so is $GA \supset GB$, hence so is $G(A \supset B) \supset (GA \supset GB)$. Since $\langle\Omega, R, \varphi\rangle$ was an arbitrarily selected historical moment of K_t, this result generally holds no matter the nature of R. Therefore $G(A \supset B) \supset (GA \supset GB)$ is valid in K_t.

(2) $P(A \,\&\, B) \supset (PA \,\&\, PB)$ (T6)

Suppose $P(A \,\&\, B)$ is true at an historical moment of K_t, say $\langle\Omega, R, \varphi\rangle$. There is, therefore, another historical moment $\langle\Omega, R, \mu\rangle$ such that both $R(\mu, \varphi)$ and

A & B is true. But then *A* is true at $\langle \Omega, R, \mu \rangle$ and *B* is true as well. Hence by the truth condition for statements of the sort *PC*, both *PA* and *PB* are true at $\langle \Omega, R, \varphi \rangle$, and so is *PA & PB*. Since $\langle \Omega, R, \varphi \rangle$ was an arbitrarily chosen historical moment of K_t this result generally holds. Therefore, *P(A & B)* $\supset$ *(PA & PB)* is valid in K_t.

   (3)   *PGA* $\supset$ *A*   (T11)

Suppose *PGA* is true at an historical moment of K_t, say $\langle \Omega, R, \varphi \rangle$. Then there is sure to be another historical moment $\langle \Omega, R, \mu \rangle$ such that both $R(\mu, \varphi)$ and *GA* is true. But then by the truth condition for statements of the sort *GB*, with *GA* true at $\langle \Omega, R, \mu \rangle$ and $R(\mu, \varphi)$, *A* is true at $\langle \Omega, R, \varphi \rangle$. Once again we can claim generality for this result and declare *PGA* $\supset$ *A* valid in K_t.

By extending arguments of the foregoing sort the reader may wish to convince himself informally that our semantics matches the deductive system one-to-one. That is, any statement *A* provable from a set *S* is also entailed by that set, every theorem is valid, every valid statement is a theorem, and if *A* is entailed by *S* then *A* is provable from *S*. Detailed proofs of these – often called soundness and completeness proofs – will be presented in Chapter 5.

Although it is not obvious from the axioms, K_t is indeed the minimal system of tense logic insofar as there are no restrictions placed on *R* in the historical moments of K_t. So *R* is free to have gaps, or, for that matter, to be any relation on Ω whatsoever. And this clearly indicates that no weaker system is possible. K_t is of interest just for this reason, its axioms and theorems indicate the statements that are logically true without any assumptions about the nature of temporal succession. The other systems of tense logic we shall study portray temporal succession as having certain features and so correspond to various views of the nature of time itself. Since these are simply extensions of K_t, all of the K_t-theorems will hold for the other systems as well.

2.2. LINEAR ENLARGEMENTS OF K_t

A linear tense logic may be intuitively conceived as a system which formally depicts temporal succession as a line. Thus, in the diagram the following statements would be true at the node marked 0: *Fp, Fq, Fr, Gr, Pp', Pq', F(p & r), Fp* ∨ *Fq*, and so forth. Note also that node 2 being to the right of 1 and, hence, in its 'future', guarantees that *Fq* is true at 1 and, consequently,

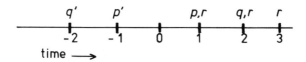

that *FFq* is true at 0. Similarly for the 'past', *PPq'* is true at 0 since *Pq'* is true at −1. It is characteristic of linear systems that whenever *FFA* is true (at an historical moment), *FA* is as well, and whenever *PPA* is true, so too is *PA*. This, as we shall see, is directly related to the relation *R* in the historical moments of linear systems being *transitive*. But this alone is not sufficient to capture linearity. A second feature of linear systems is that if *FA* and *FB* are both true, then one of three other statements must be true as well: *F(A & B)* (i.e. *A* and *B* are true at the same future historical moment), *F(A & FB)* (i.e. *A* and *B* are true at historical moments in the future such that *A*'s is earlier than *B*'s), or *F(FA & B)* (i.e. *B* is true earlier in the future than *A*). The same, as usual, holds for *PA & PB*.

This stipulation, which will turn up among the axioms of linear tense logics, prevents the situation where *FA & FB* is true at an historical moment but *A* and *B* are not true at the *same* historical moment, and neither one is in the future of the other. That is, the situation where the temporal series forks or branches, e.g.,

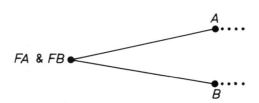

The first of the linear systems we shall discuss is *CL*, initially formulated by N. B. Cocchiarella.

(1) Axiom schemata for *CL*

A1−A7 (from K_t)

A8.   *FFA ⊃ FA*

A9.   *(FA & FB) ⊃ (F(A & B) ∨ ((F(A & FB) ∨ F(FA & B))))*

A10.   *(PA & PB) ⊃ (P(A & B) ∨ ((P(A & PB) ∨ P(PA & B))))*

(2) Rule of inference

RMP

Although the mirror image rule RMI holds in *CL* it may not be obvious from inspecting the ten axiom schemata. For A8 is not listed with its mirror image $(PPA \supset PA)$ as are all other axiom schemata we have thus far encountered. This is not an oversight, but results from the recognition that $PPA \supset PA$ is forthcoming as a theorem of *CL*.

Since all of the theorems of K_t are theorems of *CL* as well, we shall continue the numbering system of the last section.

T13. $PPA \supset PA$

Proof:

1. $FFH{\sim}A \supset FH{\sim}A$ A8
2. $FH{\sim}A \supset {\sim}A$ T12
3. $FFH{\sim}A \supset {\sim}A$ SC2, RMP (1, 2)
4. $H(FFH{\sim}A \supset {\sim}A)$ RH (3)
5. $HFFH{\sim}A \supset H{\sim}A$ A3, SC2, RMP (4)
6. $FH{\sim}A \supset HFFH{\sim}A$ A4
7. $FH{\sim}A \supset H{\sim}A$ SC2, RMP (5, 6)
8. $H(FH{\sim}A \supset H{\sim}A)$ RH (7)
9. $HFH{\sim}A \supset HH{\sim}A$ A3, SC2, RMP (8)
10. $H{\sim}A \supset HFH{\sim}A$ A4
11. $H{\sim}A \supset HH{\sim}A$ SC2, RMP (9, 10)
12. ${\sim}HH{\sim}A \supset {\sim}H{\sim}A$ SC1, RMP (11)
13. $PPA \supset PA$ Def. P/H, REQ, SC15 (12)

T14. $P(FA \& FB) \supset (PF(A \& B) \vee (PF(A \& FB) \vee PF(FA \& B)))$

Proof:

1. $(FA \& FB) \supset (F(A \& B) \vee (F(A \& FB)$
    $\vee F(B \& FA)))$ A9
2. $H((FA \& FB) \supset (F(A \& B) \vee (F(A \& FB)$
    $\vee F(B \& FA))))$ RH (1)
3. $P(FA \& FB) \supset P(F(A \& B) \vee (F(A \& FB)$
    $\vee F(B \& FA)))$ T2, SC2, RMP, (2)
4. $P(F(A \& B) \vee (F(A \& FB) \vee F(B \& FA)))$
    $\supset (PF(A \& B) \vee (PF(A \& FB)$
    $\vee PF(B \& FA)))$ T10, SC2, RMP, (3)

5. $P(FA \& FB) \supset (PF(A \& B) \vee (PF(A \& FB)$
     $\vee PF(B \& FA)))$ SC2, RMP, (3, 4)

T15. $F(PA \& PB) \supset (FP(A \& B) \vee (FP(A \& PB) \vee FP(B \& PA)))$

Proof: By RMI and T14.

T16.[7] $\sim(PF(\sim A \& (GA \& (A \& HA))) \vee (PF(F \sim A \& (GA \& (A \& HA)))$
      $\vee PF(\sim A \& F(GA \& (A \& HA)))))$

Proof:

1. $\sim(\sim A \& (GA \& (A \& HA)))$ SC16
2. $H\sim(\sim A \& (GA \& (A \& HA)))$ RH (1)
3. $GH\sim(\sim A \& (GA \& (A \& HA)))$ RG (2)
4. $\sim FP(\sim A \& (GA \& (A \& HA)))$ Def. F/G, P/H (3)
5. $\sim(\sim HA \& (GA \& (A \& HA)))$ SC17, REQ, SC16
6. $H\sim(\sim HA \& (GA \& (A \& HA)))$ RH (5)
7. $GH\sim(\sim HA \& (GA \& (A \& HA)))$ RG (6)
8. $\sim FP(P \sim A \& (GA \& (A \& HA)))$ Def. F/G, P/H (7)
9. $\sim GA \supset (\sim GA \vee \sim(A \& HA))$ SC3
10. $\sim GA \supset \sim(GA \& (A \& HA))$ SC6, SC15 REQ (9)
11. $H(\sim GA \supset \sim(GA \& (A \& HA)))$ RH (10)
12. $H \sim GA \supset H\sim(GA \& (A \& HA))$ A2, SC2, RMP (11)
13. $\sim H\sim(GA \& (A \& HA)) \supset \sim H \sim GA$ SC1, SC2, RMP (12)
14. $\sim H \sim GA \supset A$ T11, Def. P/H
15. $P(GA \& (A \& HA)) \supset A$ SC2, RMP (13, 14),
                                      Def. P/H

16. $\sim A \supset \sim P(GA \& (A \& HA)))$ SC1, RMP (15)
17. $\sim(\sim A \& P(GA \& (A \& HA)))$ SC18, REQ (16)
18. $H\sim(\sim A \& P(GA \& (A \& HA)))$ RH (17)
19. $GH\sim(\sim A \& P(GA \& (A \& HA)))$ RG (18)
20. $\sim FP(\sim A \& P(GA \& (A \& HA)))$ Def. F/G, P/H (19)
21. $\sim FP(P \sim A \& (GA \& (A \& HA)))$
    $\& \sim FP(\sim A \& P(GA \& (A \& HA)))$ SC10, RMP (8, 20)
22. $\sim(FP(P \sim A \& (GA \& (A \& HA)))$
    $\vee FP(\sim A \& P(GA \& (A \& HA))))$ SC13, SC14, SC15 REQ
                                      (21)

23. $\sim FP(\sim A \& (GA \& (A \& HA)))$
    $\& \sim(FP(P \sim A \& (GA \& (A \& HA)))$
    $\vee FP(\sim A \& P(GA \& (A \& HA))))$ SC10, RMP (4, 22)

24. $\sim(FP(\sim A \;\&\; (GA \;\&\; (A \;\&\; HA)))$
    $\vee \;(FP(P\sim A \;\&\; (GA \;\&\; (A \;\&\; HA)))$
    $\vee \;FP(\sim A \;\&\; P(GA \;\&\; (A \;\&\; HA))))$ SC13, SC14, SC15, REQ
                                                                  (23)

25. $\sim(PF(\sim A \;\&\; (GA \;\&\; (A \;\&\; HA)))$
    $\vee \;(PF(F\sim A \;\&\; (GA \;\&\; (A \;\&\; HA)))$
    $\vee \;PF(\sim A \;\&\; F(GA \;\&\; (A \;\&\; HA)))))$ RMI, REQ, SC17, (24)

T17. $(GA \;\&\; (A \;\&\; HA)) \supset HGA$

Proof:
1. $(GA \;\&\; (A \;\&\; HA)) \supset HF(GA \;\&\; (A \;\&\; HA))$ A4
2. $(HF(GA \;\&\; (A \;\&\; HA)) \;\&\; PF\sim A)$
   $\supset P(F(GA \;\&\; (A \;\&\; HA)) \;\&\; F\sim A)$ T2
3. $P(F(GA \;\&\; (A \;\&\; HA)) \;\&\; F\sim A)$
   $\supset (PF(\sim A \;\&\; (GA \;\&\; (A \;\&\; HA)))$
   $\vee \;PF(\sim A \;\&\; F(GA \;\&\; (A \;\&\; HA)))$
   $\vee \;PF(F\sim A \;\&\; (GA \;\&\; (A \;\&\; HA)))))$ T14, SC18, REQ
4. $\sim(PF(\sim A \;\&\; (GA \;\&\; (A \;\&\; HA)))$
   $\vee \;(PF(\sim A \;\&\; F(GA \;\&\; (A \;\&\; HA)))$
   $\vee \;PF(F\sim A \;\&\; (GA \;\&\; (A \;\&\; HA))))$ T16, SC19, REQ
5. $\sim P(F(GA \;\&\; (A \;\&\; HA)) \;\&\; F\sim A)$ SC20, RMP (3, 4)
6. $\sim(HF(GA \;\&\; (A \;\&\; HA)) \;\&\; PF\sim A)$ SC20, RMP (2, 5)
7. $HF(GA \;\&\; (A \;\&\; HA)) \supset \sim PF\sim A$ SC21, REQ (6)
8. $HF(GA \;\&\; (A \;\&\; HA)) \supset HGA$ Def. P/H, F/G (7)
9. $(GA \;\&\; (A \;\&\; HA)) \supset HGA$ SC2, RMP, (1, 8)

T18. $(GA \;\&\; (A \;\&\; HA)) \supset GHA$

Proof: By RMI and T17, together with SC17 and REQ.

Although *CL* is usually formulated as above, an alternative axiomatization replaces A9 and A10 by T17 and T18.[8] Proofs of about the same complexity as that of T17 can be found in the literature which show A9 and A10 as theorems of this other version of *CL*.[9]

As expected, the semantics for *CL* differs from that for K_t only in specifying properties for the relation R in the *CL*-historical moments. One property is required for each axiom beyond those of K_t, so three properties in all are specified for R. These are as follows:

P1. $(\forall x)(\forall y)(\forall z)((R(x,y) \,\&\, R(y,z)) \supset R(x,z))$

P2. $(\forall x)(\forall y)(\forall z)((R(x,y) \,\&\, R(x,z)) \supset ((x=y) \vee (R(y,z)$
$\vee R(z,y))))$

P3. $(\forall x)(\forall y)(\forall z)((R(y,x) \,\&\, R(z,x)) \supset ((y=z) \vee (R(z,y)$
$\vee R(y,z))))$

P1 is often called the property of *transitivity*, P2 is called *right-linearity*, and P3 is called *left-linearity*.

Why *CL* is known as a linear tense logic emerges from a careful appraisal of P2 and P3. For these two properties of *R* guarantee that no forks or branches occur in the temporal series in either direction. Two properties are required because, at any given point, the non-branchingness of the future is independent from the non-branchingness of the past.

It may be helpful to return, on this point, to the diagram on p. 25, wherein the temporal series is depicted as forking. Since the nodes of the diagram are truth-value assignments (members of Ω) and, hence, have names, let them be as below:

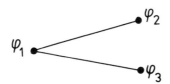

With *R* as the temporal successor relation, we would have in this case both $R(\varphi_1, \varphi_2)$ (i.e. the top branch) and $R(\varphi_1, \varphi_3)$ (the bottom branch). But we do not have any of the three disjuncts that P2 requires; viz. $(\varphi_2 = \varphi_3)$, $R(\varphi_2, \varphi_3)$, and $R(\varphi_3, \varphi_2)$. As noted earlier, the antecedent of A9 can obtain in such a situation although the consequent $(F(A \,\&\, B) \vee (F(A \,\&\, FB) \vee F(FA \,\&\, B)))$ need not. Thus the correspondence between P2 and A9 is quite obvious. And the same would hold for P3 and A10.

Even though *CL* is the linear tense logic most frequently encountered in the literature, there are several others which are properly viewed as extensions of *CL*. These posit additional properties for *R* such as non-endingness (in both directions), density, and circularity. Non-endingness in future and past are obtained with the properties

P4. $(\forall x)(\exists y)R(x,y)$

P5. $(\forall x)(\exists y)R(y,x)$

and density is obtained with the single property

P6. $(\forall x)(\forall y)(\exists z)(R(x,y) \supset (R(x,z) \& R(z,y)))$.

However, when it comes to circularity, the requisite properties are:

P7. $(\forall x)R(x,x)$

P8. $(\forall x)(\forall y)(R(x,y) \supset R(y,x))$

P7 is often called *reflexivity* and P8 *symmetry*. These two properties cannot merely be added to P1–P6 without a great deal of redundancy. For it is easily shown that P7 and P8, together with P1 (transitivity), imply all of the others. P7 alone implies P4–P6, and P2–P3 are implied by the conjunction of P1, P7, and P8. Consequently, the properties of R in the circular system are P1, P7, and P8.

To turn to the axiomatic formulation of these systems, the non-ending linear tense logic is called *SL* and is attributed to Dana Scott. Its axioms are as follows:

(1) Axioma Schemata for *SL*

A1–A10 *(CL)*

A11. $GA \supset FA$

A12. $HA \supset PA$

(2) Rule of Inference

        RMP

Some of the theorems of *SL* are given below.

T19. $\sim FA \supset F \sim A$

Proof:
1. $G \sim A \supset F \sim A$ A11
2. $\sim FA \supset F \sim A$ Def. F/G (1)

T20. $\sim PA \supset P \sim A$

Proof: By RMI and T19.

T21. $F(A \supset A)$

Proof:

1. $A \supset A$	SC22
2. $G(A \supset A)$	RG (1)
3. $G(A \supset A) \supset F(A \supset A)$	A11
4. $F(A \supset A)$	SC2, RMP (2, 3)

T22. $P(A \supset A)$

Proof: By RMI and T21.

Since R in the *SL*-historical moments has P4 and P5, as previously noted, there cannot be a 'last' or 'first' historical moment in the series, if this is understood to mean one which does not bear the relation R to any other. However, we do not have a guarantee of an infinite series here, although it may seem so, because we do not rule out historical moments bearing the relation to themselves (i.e. reflexive relations). To do so, e.g., by adding the property $(\forall x) \sim R(x, x)$, would have the unfortunate consequence of imposing a property on R which is inexpressible in terms of the tense operators. And this would break the symmetry which holds otherwise between the syntactical and semantical formulations. That is to say, our semantics would no longer serve as an adequate interpretation of the axiomatic system, and, to put it the other way, the axiomatic system would fail to represent the semantics.

A. N. Prior is credited with the discovery of the dense linear tense logic which we shall call *PL*. It adds only one axiom schema to those of *SL* as follows.

(1). Axiom Schemata for *PL*

A1–A12 (*SL*)

A13. $FA \supset FFA$

(2). Rule of Inference

RMP

Once again, although no mirror image is listed for A13, RMI holds for the system insofar as $PA \supset PPA$ is forthcoming as a theorem.

T23. $PA \supset PPA$

Proof:

1. $FHH{\sim}A \supset FFHH{\sim}A$	A13
2. $FHH{\sim}A \supset H{\sim}A$	T12
3. $G(FHH{\sim}A \supset H{\sim}A)$	RG (2)
4. $FFHH{\sim}A \supset FH{\sim}A$	T1, SC2, RMP (3)
5. $FHH{\sim}A \supset FH{\sim}A$	SC2, RMP (1, 4)
6. $FH{\sim}A \supset {\sim}A$	T12
7. $FHH{\sim}A \supset {\sim}A$	SC2, RMP (5, 6)
8. $H(FHH{\sim}A \supset {\sim}A)$	RH (7)
9. $HFHH{\sim}A \supset H{\sim}A$	A3, SC2, RMP (8)
10. $HH{\sim}A \supset HFHH{\sim}A$	A4
11. $HH{\sim}A \supset H{\sim}A$	SC2, RMP (9, 10)
12. ${\sim}H{\sim}A \supset {\sim}HH{\sim}A$	SC1, RMP (11)
13. $PA \supset PPA$	Def. P/H

T24. $HHA \supset HA$

Proof:

1. $P{\sim}A \supset PP{\sim}A$	T23
2. ${\sim}PP{\sim}A \supset {\sim}P{\sim}A$	SC1, RMP (1)
3. $HHA \supset HA$	Def. P/H

T25. $GGA \supset GA$

Proof: By RMI and T24.

T26. $GA \supset GPA$

Proof:

1. $A \supset GPA$	A5
2. $GA \supset GGPA$	RG $\supset$ (2)
3. $GGPA \supset GPA$	T25
4. $GA \supset GPA$	SC2, RMP (2, 3)

T27. $HA \supset HFA$

Proof: By RMI and T26.

The extra axiom required for $PL - FA \supset FFA$ — corresponds to the property of 'density' for R (i.e., P6) in PL-historical moments. For example, suppose FA is true at $\langle \Omega, R, \varphi \rangle$, in which case A is true at some $\langle \Omega, R, \mu \rangle$

such that $R(\varphi, \mu)$. Then A13 insures that 'between' φ and μ there is another moment, say φ', such that FA is also true at $\langle \Omega, R, \varphi' \rangle$. If there were no such moment as φ', FFA might turn out false at $\langle \Omega, R, \varphi \rangle$. But note that although R has P6, it may not be actually a dense relation. Since reflexivity cannot be ruled out for R in PL-historical moments, φ' might just be φ or μ.

Finally, the circular system, here called PCr and also due to Prior, is axiomatized in a somewhat different fashion from the others we have been treating.

(1) Axiom Schemata

A1–A7 (K_t)

A8. $FFA \supset FA$

A14. $GA \supset A$

A15. $GA \supset HA$

(2) Rule of Inference

    RMP

The strangeness of these axioms is somewhat alleviated by considering the time series as diagrammed as below.

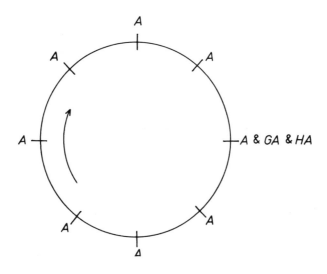

Note indeed, that *GA*'s truth does entail that of *HA* (and vice versa), so that in circular time *G* and *H* become logically equivalent, as do *F* and *P*. Furthermore, in accord with A14, if either *GA* or *HA* holds (at a *PCr*-historical moment) then so must *A*.

As the reader may have already conjectured, *PCr* contains all of the other tense logics as subsystems. To show this we will prove A9—A13 in *PCr*. In the case of A9 and A10, proof of their equivalents (T17 and T18) shall be given for the sake of brevity. Note that we can only presume T1—T13 as holding in *PCr*. Hence we shall adopt a separate numbering system for the theorems to be set out here.

Tlc.   *FGA ⊃ A*

Proof:

1. *GA ⊃ HA*	A15
2. *G(GA ⊃ HA)*	RG (1)
3. *FGA ⊃ FHA*	T1, SC2, RMP (2)
4. *FHA ⊃ A*	T12
5. *FGA ⊃ A*	SC2, RMP (3, 4)

T2c.   *PHA ⊃ A*

Proof:

1. *GP~A ⊃ HP~A*	A15
2. *~A ⊃ GP~A*	A5
3. *~A ⊃ HP~A*	SC2, RMP (1, 2)
4. *~HP~A ⊃ ~~A*	SC1, RMP (3)
5. *~~P~P~A ⊃ ~~A*	Def. P/H (4)
6. *~~PHA ⊃ ~~A*	Def. P/H (5)
7. *PHA ⊃ A*	SC15, REQ (6)

T3c.   *HA ≡ GA*

1. *GA ⊃ HA*	A15
2. *PHA ⊃ A*	T2c.
3. *GPHA ⊃ GA*	RG⊃ (2)
4. *HA ⊃ GPHA*	A5
5. *HA ⊃ GA*	SC2, RMP (3, 4)
6. *HA ≡ GA*	SC12, RMP (1, 5)

T4c.   *HA ⊃ A*

Proof: By A14, T3c and REQ.

With T3c and T4c in hand, we can henceforth make use of RMI which we are now assured holds for *PCr*.

T5c. $(GA \& (A \& HA)) \supset GHA$ (T17 = A9)

Proof:

1. $GA \supset HA$	A15
2. $GGA \supset GHA$	RG$\supset$ (1)
3. $FF{\sim}A \supset F{\sim}A$	A8
4. ${\sim}F{\sim}A \supset {\sim}FF{\sim}A$	SC1, RMP (3)
5. $GA \supset GGA$	Def. F/G (4)
6. $GA \supset GHA$	SC2, RMP (2, 5)
7. $(GA \supset GHA) \supset ((GA \& (A \& HA)) \supset GHA)$	SC23
8. $(GA \& (A \& HA)) \supset GHA$	SC2, RMP (6, 7)

T6c. $(GA \& (A \& HA)) \supset HGA$ (T18 = A10)

Proof: By T5c and RMI, together with SC17 and REQ.

T7c. $GA \supset FA$ (A11)

Proof:

1. $GA \supset A$	A14
2. $G{\sim}A \supset {\sim}A$	A14
3. ${\sim}{\sim}A \supset {\sim}G{\sim}A$	SC1, RMP (2)
4. $A \supset FA$	Def. F/G, REQ, SC15, RMP (3)
5. $GA \supset FA$	SC2, RMP (1, 4)

T8c. $HA \supset PA$ (A12)

Proof: By T7c. and RMI.

T9c. $FA \supset FFA$ (A13)

Proof:

1. $GG{\sim}A \supset G{\sim}A$	A14
2. ${\sim}G{\sim}A \supset {\sim}GG{\sim}A$	SC1, RMP (1)
3. $FA \supset FFA$	Def. F/G (2)

With *R* in the *PCr* historical moments defined as reflexive, transitive and symmetrical (i.e. P7, P1, and P8, respectively), we can act as though every member of Ω bears the relation R to every other. Hence R is dispensable in the PCr-historical moments which can be portrayed as just pairs of the sort $\langle \Omega, \varphi \rangle$.[10] This gives rise to slightly altered truth conditions for statements of the sorts FA, PA, GA, and HA, as given below.

(4′) A is of the sort FB, B is true at some member μ of Ω,

(5′) A is of the sort PB, B is true at some member μ of Ω,

(6′) A is of the sort GB, B, is true at every member μ of Ω, and

(7′) A is of the sort HB, B is true at every member μ of Ω.

From these truth conditions, one can see that there is no longer any need for both past and future tense operators. So this system could be equivalently formulated with a single (primitive) operator, say F, and G would be available by definition, and P and H by equivalences of the sort T3c.

NOTES

[1] For alternative formulations, the history, and additional information about this and the other tense logics in this chapter consult Prior, 1967, Appendix I, and *passim*.

[2] One often sees inference rules of the sort 'if $\vdash A$ then $\vdash GA$' and 'if $\vdash A$ then $\vdash HA$' in place of these last two axiom schemata (for example in Prior, 1967). However, for metalogical purposes these schemata are preferable. We introduce the rule form as derived rules of inference on pp. 19–20.

[3] It is easy to show that if $\sim(p \supset p)$ is provable from a set S, then so are A and $\sim A$, for any statement A of the system. Hence, this definition amounts to saying that a set is inconsistent if and only if all contradictions are provable from the set.

[4] Proof of each of these is given in Lemma 1 of Chapter 5.

[5] I.e., the truth-value of A on (the truth-value assignment) φ is 1.

[6] In Chapter 5 it will be shown that we need only a denumerable subset for our purposes, and, hence, that our indices could well be the positive integers.

[7] The proofs of T14–T16 owe much to Rescher and Urquhart. These theorems are included so as to make the proofs of T17 and T18 simpler.

[8] See Prior, 1967, Appendix I.

[9] See Prior, 1967, p. 52.

[10] Because R has P7, P1, and P8, it partitions Ω into equivalence classes. From the standpoint of *validity*, therefore, R is superfluous in PCr-historical moments, as the reader may wish to verify. Those familiar with the modal logic S_s will recognize this point.

CHAPTER 3

BRANCHING TENSE LOGIC AND
TEMPORAL MODALITY

3.1. BRANCHING TENSE LOGICS

Branching tense logics are simply described from the axiomatic perspective: they lack one, or both, of axioms A9 and A10. The reader will recall these schemata to have been singled out as 'axioms of linearity' in Chapter 2. But a more intuitive characterization is given in semantic terms: the temporal orders represented by such logics permit forks, or branches.

The basic system of branching tense logic is Cocchiarella's system CR.[1]

(1) Axiom Schemata for CR

A1–A7 (from K_t)

A8. $FFA \supset FA$

(2) Rule of Inference

   RMP

CR is just an extension of K_t formed by the addition of A8 (semantically: transitivity), hence the theorems of CR will include all of T1–T12. In addition, those theorems provable from K_t plus A8 are theorems of CR as well; e.g., T13 and T16. Note the branching aspect of CR (and of the other branching systems) comes, in a sense, by default, since the axioms do not *require* the corresponding models to depict branching temporal orders.

A second system, between CR and CL as it turns out, adds A10 to the axiom schemata of CR. This allows branching only to the right (i.e., in the future). Rescher and Urquhart have dubbed this system K_b.[2]

(1) Axiom Schemata for K_b

A1–A8 (from CR)

A10. $(PA \ \& \ PB) \supset (P(A \ \& \ B) \vee ((P(A \ \& \ PB) \vee P(PA \ \& \ B)))$

(2) Rule of Inference

   RMP

As expected, all *CR*-theorems are also K_b-theorems. In addition, T18 is a theorem of K_b since its proof depends only upon A1−A8 and A10.

Further enlargements of *CR*, paralleling those to *CL* in Section 2.2, are available here, although the literature on tense logic has given them little attention. Hence, any of A11 (*GA ⊃ FA*), A12 (*HA ⊃ PA*), and A13 (*FA ⊃ FFA*) can be utilized to extend K_b (or *CR*) to suit a variety of purposes.

CR preserves the mirror-image property found to characterize all of the systems discussed in Chapter 2, but K_b does not. Hence RMI is a rule only for *CR*, and not for the other branching systems. Proofs analogous to those in Section 2.1 can be supplied in both systems for the remaining derived rules: RG, RH, RG ⊃, and RH ⊃.

Branching tense logics were originally developed for semantic purposes, and, indeed, are more interesting when studied in that light. Both *CR* and K_b have semantics formulated in terms of the *historical moments* of Chapter 2, i.e., triples of the sort $\langle \Omega, R, \varphi \rangle$. The relation R in the historical moments of *CR* is required only to have property P1 (transitivity), whereas R in K_b-historical moments has both P1 and P3 (left-linearity). The truth conditions for the various connectives and operators are, in both cases, defined as in Chapter 2. The same holds for the definitions of satisfiability, validity, and entailment.

Since the only required property for R in *CR*-historical moments is transitivity, the temporal order represented by *CR* might appear as below.

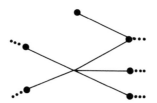

K_b, on the other hand, requiring R to be both transitive and left-linear, could be diagrammed:

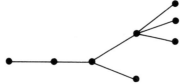

In both systems, FA is interpreted as 'A somewhere in the branches to the right of the origin (present)', and GA is interpreted as 'A everywhere in the branches to the right of the origin'. PA and HA, for CR, are handled analogously. In the case of K_b, however, PA and HA are interpreted as in the linear systems of Chapter 2.

To further illustrate the differences between the systems, the set

$$\{FPA, \sim A \,\&\, (H\sim A \,\&\, G\sim A)\}$$

(i.e., A will have been the case, A hasn't yet been the case and never will be the case) is satisfiable in CR, as the following diagram shows.

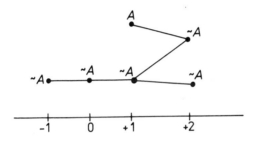

However, the linear shape of the past rules out this situation in K_b. Or to put the point in a different way, by T18 (of K_b)

$$\{\sim A \,\&\, (H\sim A \,\&\, G\sim A)\} \vdash GH\sim A \quad (= \sim FPA)$$

An intuitive understanding for the members of Ω was suggested in Chapter 1, which may require revision here. Recall the (indexed) truth-value assignments making up Ω were thought of as representatives of temporal world states; past, present, and future. To continue to hold this view, apropos of the historical moments of CR and K_b, necessitates the additional doctrine that there may be *several* such world states at each successive interval of time. Indeed, CR is often given just this interpretation, which some suggest fits the Minkowskian view of (causal) relativistic time in contemporary physics.[3]

As far as K_b is concerned, since branching occurs only in the future, the past and future are not symmetrical. This has brought forth yet another understanding of Ω and its members. Instead of being *actual* temporal world states, as in the other systems, take the members of Ω to be *possible* temporal world states, only *some* of which achieve actuality in the course of time. This yields a quite natural understanding of the different 'logics' of the past and future found in K_b. The past consists, at any historical moment, exclusively of actualized world states, whereas the future is still in the realm of the merely possible. To take an example, consider the diagram

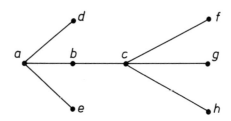

If node c is taken as the *present* world state, then the *past* consists of nodes a and b, the future possibilities are nodes f, g, and h. Nodes d and e were *once* future possibilities, specifically when node a was the present, but are no longer possibilities at all. Time has passed them by, one might say. Generally speaking, the only world states in the past of node c are those which *were present* at some time or other.[4]

One of the adjustments which seems to be called for by this shift in the understanding of the membership of Ω is our ordinary language translation of the future tense operators. Statements of the sort FA in K_b – under this view, at least – are closer to 'It possibly will be the case that A' than to the 'It will be the case that A' of the linear systems. GA would then become 'It necessarily will always be the case that A', or something of this sort. These readings for F and G provide a reasonable interpretation for the members of the K_b-satisfiable set:

$$\{PFA, \sim A \ \& \ (H \sim A \ \& \ G \sim A)\}$$

diagrammatically:

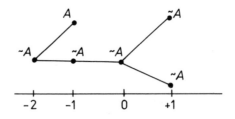

This simply asserts that although it *was* possible that A, it never actually was the case, and cannot be in the future. Note how awkward a reading of these statements would be under the usual renderings of F and G.

Concrete examples of the situation depicted above are not hard to come by. In September 1972, to take one such case, it was possible that Richard Nixon would lose the upcoming Presidential election, but it didn't happen, and, of course, now won't ever happen.

Should the reader feel we have gained something by this 'modalization' of the future operators F and G in K_b, he ought to realize we have lost as well. For although possibility and necessity (in their temporal senses) are express-ible in K_b under this interpretation, the plain 'It will be the case that' is not.[5] Even if the formal apparatus of K_b were enriched so as to include metric indices on the future tense operators, this would still hold.

To illustrate the point, suppose we utilize a metric scale which ranks the nodes in a branching model (see the diagram below), and then take $F^n A$ to mean 'A at every n-node', where the n-nodes are all the nodes of rank n $(n > 0)$. Thus, $F^2 A$ would be:

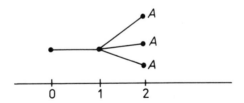

Then, take $(\exists n)F^n$ as a replacement for the standard F (so long as the vari-able of quantification is presumed to be a positive integer). G then becomes $(\forall n)F^n$, which is, of course, the dual of $(\exists n)F^n$. Whereas our original inter-pretation for F in a branching system seemed too *weak* to capture the ordin-ary sense of *will*, this metric version of F is really too *strong*. It has the flavour of 'It necessarily will be that, n units hence'. For even branches which are *not* actualized must have an occurrence of A, if $(\exists n)F^n A$ is the case at the origin.

In the next section we shall look at this problem from two other perspec-tives, both of which try to deliver means of expressing the standard future tense and some sort of temporal modality within the same system.

3.2. TEMPORAL MODALITY

In this section we shall be concerned with methods of achieving what proved so difficult in the case of K_b, viz. the expressibility of both the standard future tense and some modal future tense within a single system of tense logic. As we shall discover, much depends on how we construe the modalities of possibility and necessity.

1. A first alternative is to follow the ancient logicians and define possibility and necessity -- henceforth represented by the *modal operators M* (It is possible that) and *L* (It is necessary that) -- in terms of the tense operators already discussed. To be specific, we can follow the Stoic logician *Diodorus of Chronos* and understand the possible to be that which either is (now) or will be, and the necessary as that which is both now the case and will always be. This leads to the *Diodorian* definitions of the modal operators:

Dla. $MA =_{df} A \lor FA$

Dlb. $LA =_{df} A \& GA$

Either one of Dla and Dlb is sufficient to define both operators since they are duals (just as F and G, and P and H). Hence the equivalences

$$MA \equiv \sim L \sim A$$

$$LA \equiv \sim M \sim A$$

are preserved by these definitions. On the other hand, we can follow *Aristotle* who defined possibility and necessity in terms of past, present, and future. The *Aristotelian* definitions are:

D2a. $MA =_{df} PA \lor (A \lor FA)$

D2b. $LA =_{df} HA \& (A \& GA)$

Once again, the duality of M and L is preserved.[6]

Utilizing the Diodorian or the Aristotelian conception of temporal modality permits the introduction of the modal operators into any system of tense logic as defined signs. This, it should be noted, does not add anything to the system (in the strict sense), but does allow for a different grouping of the theorems. If we restrict our attention to the theorems of a given system, say K_t, whose *only* operators are M and L, this yields the *modal fragment* of the system. In many cases, as for example in K_t, the modal fragment for either the Diodorian or Aristotelian modalities will be one of the well known modal logics. When M and L are defined by Dla and Dlb, the modal fragment of K_t is equivalent to the modal system M (or T). When D2a and D2b are used, the modal fragment is the system B. To illustrate this point, standard axiomatizations of M and B are provided below.

M: $(MA =_{df} {\sim}L{\sim}A)$

A1. A, where A is a tautology

M1. $LA \supset A$

M2. $L(A \supset B) \supset (LA \supset LB)$

M3. LA, where A is a theorem

RMP.

B: $(MA =_{df} {\sim}L{\sim}A)$

A1. A, where A is a tautology

M1–M3 (M)

M4. $MLA \supset LA$

RMP

The modal fragments for all of the tense logics thus far treated are given in the following table. (Standard axiomatizations of the modal systems are gathered in Appendix II)

Tense logic[7]	Diodorian fragment	Aristotelian fragment
K_t	M	B
CR	S_4	B
K_b	S_4	B
CL	$S_{4.3}$	S_5
SL	$S_{4.3}$	S_5
PL	$S_{4.3}$	S_5
PC_r	S_5	S_5

Although treating modality as definable in terms of the tense operators provides the expressibility we earlier desired, it is not as satisfactory as one might want. For in any tense logic having $FFA \supset FA$ among its theorems (i.e., CR and its extensions), the following will also be a theorem

$$FMA \supset FA$$

given the Diodorian definition of M. But this is clearly counter-intuitive: 'It will be possible that A' does not seem to imply 'It will be the case that A'. A similar anomaly crops up under the Aristotelian definition of L. In all tense logics, the statement

$$FLA \supset A$$

counts as a theorem. This, of course, says 'If it will be necessary that A, then A is now the case', which also seems counter-intuitive.

The proofs of these two theorems are as follows.

(a) $\vdash FMA \supset FA$

1. $F(A \vee FA) \supset (FA \vee FFA)$	T9
2. $FFA \supset FA$	A8
3. $(FA \vee FFA) \supset ((FFA \supset FA) \supset FA)$	SC24
4. $F(A \vee FA) \supset ((FFA \supset FA) \supset FA)$	SC2, RMP (1, 3)
5. $(F(A \vee FA) \supset ((FFA \supset FA) \supset FA)) \supset$ $((FFA \supset FA) \supset (F(A \vee FA) \supset FA))$	SC25
6. $(FFA \supset FA) \supset (F(A \vee FA) \supset FA)$	SC2, RMP (5, 4)
7. $F(A \vee FA) \supset FA$	RMP (2, 6)
8. $FMA \supset FA$	Dla. (7)

(b) $\vdash FLA \supset A$

1. $F(HA \& (A \& GA)) \supset (FHA \& F(A \& GA))$	T5
2. $(FHA \& F(A \& GA)) \supset FHA$	SC7
3. $F(HA \& (A \& GA)) \supset FHA$	SC2, RMP (1, 2)
4. $FHA \supset A$	T12
5. $F(HA \& (A \& GA)) \supset A$	SC2, RMP (3, 4)
6. $FLA \supset A$	D2b. (5)

Even with the additional modal operators introduced by means of the Diodorian or Aristotelian definitions, the dilemma suggested at the end of Section 3.1 remains. In branching tense logics (i.e., CR and K_b), the force of F and G is still somewhat modal, and the elusiveness of 'It *will* be the case that' persists. In the linear systems, M and L fail to be very satisfactory, due to the provability of *FMA* $\supset A$ and *FLA* $\supset A$ discussed above. This brings us to a second manner of handling the difficulty.

2. It is an ancient doctrine (also found in Aristotle) that *temporal possibility* applies only to the future. On this view, what has already been the case, or is now the case, is necessarily so, at least from the present perspective. To illustrate the point consider the statement:

Lincoln was shot in 1865.

Now (in 1976) it cannot be otherwise that Lincoln was shot in 1865, so it naturally seems false to say that it now is possible that he wasn't shot in 1865. The same sort of argument also applies to true, present tense statements, e.g., 'The weather today is sunny'. If the weather today is sunny, then it cannot (today) be otherwise, hence it is not possible (today) that the weather isn't sunny. Of course, it *once* was possible (i.e., prior to 1865) that Lincoln would not be shot in 1865, and it *once* was possible that the sun wouldn't shine today. But, it should be noted, these possibilities are future possibilities relative to a time interval prior to 1865 (in the first case) and prior to today (in the second).

The situation we have described here, it turns out, is precisely that depicted by the branching tense logic K_b. Take *F* to read 'It will be possible that', *G* to read 'It necessarily will be that' and take *P* and *H* as usual. Since the past is linear no possibilities exist other than what in fact has occurred. *From the present perspective*, no alternatives to the present are available either. In the future, however, there are alternatives at every interval, and, hence, possibilities. Indeed, it was this realization (in Section 3.1) which prompted our comment that in K_b, no ordinary sense of 'It *will* be the case that' is available. What is clear from this consideration is that any adequate rendering of the temporal modalities will have to function as do *F* and *G* in K_b (or, as we shall presently suggest, one of its extensions). But what is equally clear, is that the future tense operator *F* (and, hence, *G*) in order to capture the standard sense of 'It will be the case that', must function as *F* does in the *linear* systems. Thus, the crux of the problem is how to have in a single system both a branching interpretation for the modal operators and a linear interpretation for the tense operators.

It was Prior who originally suggested a solution to this problem, although the details of our account are also due to Davis, McKim, and Thomason.[8] The

basic insight (due to Prior) is that each branch in a system such as that portrayed by K_b is, itself, a linear series. Hence the branching model can be considered as a collection of partially overlapping linear models. Suppose, as in
the diagram below, we singled out one branch, say the top branch, and considered it the *actual future*. By this we mean that it will be *the* series of future
states of the world, and the other branches, although possible, will not be
actualized.

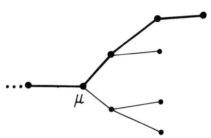

Care must be taken here to insure that this ploy doesn't lapse into incoher-
ency. For if the top branch is *already* the future series, then it cannot (now)
be otherwise that this is the case, and, hence, the world states on the other
branches are no more possible than those in the past. In effect, this would
cause a collapse back to a linear conception of temporal succession. Against
this line of argument, it must be urged that it is an incontrovertible fact that
one of the branches emanating from the origin in the above diagram will be
that which is actual. The catch is that we cannot know (and, hence, cannot
say) which one it is on pain of losing the branching conception of the future.
Hence we shall make use of a tactic of Prior's. Instead of the claim that a certain branch is the *actual* future, choose one *arbitrarily* and call it the *prima
facie future* of that particular historical moment. This done, the rest is
straightforward. Take, for example, the upper branch in the diagram above to
be the *prima facie* future. *FA* is true at the origin (μ) if and only if *A* is true
somewhere along the branch, *GA* is true if and only if *A* is true at every point
on the branch, and *M* and *L* (for the two modalites) have exactly the same
truth-conditions as those for *F* and *G*, respectively, in the original version of
K_b. Then, since validity is defined in terms of *all* historical moments, all the
possibilities for *prima facie* futures will crop up, insuring the generality that
we seek. Let us now turn to the detailed formulation of this system which is
called *OT*.[9]

In addition to the usual signs and formation rules common to all of the tense logics treated so far, *OT* has an extra' primitive operator *M* ('It will possibly be the case that') and an extra clause in the definition of statement-hood. *L* occurs among the defined signs of *OT* as the dual of *M* (= $\sim M \sim$) and is read 'It will necessarily be the case that'. Turning then to the axioms of *OT*, they are as follows.

(1) Axioms for *OT*

A1–A12 (*SL*)

A16. $L(A \supset B) \supset (LA \supset LB)$

A17. $MMA \supset MA$

A18. LA, where *A* is an axiom

A19. $LA \supset GA$

A20. $A \supset LPA$, where *A* contains no occurrences of *F*

(2) Rule of Inference

   RMP

Since the *F*–*P*–*G*–*H* component of *OT* is just Scott's system *SL* (for endless, beginningless linear time), we should expect all of T1–T27 to be theorems of *OT*. In addition, although RMI is not provable *in general* as a rule of inference for *OT*, a restricted version RMI* is; i.e., If $\vdash A$, and *A* contains no modal operators, then $\vdash MI(A)$.

Proofs of some other *OT* theorems are given below.

T28. $FA \supset MA$

Proof:

1. $L \sim A \supset G \sim A$	A19
2. $(L \sim A \supset G \sim A) \supset (\sim G \sim A \supset \sim L \sim A)$	SC1
3. $\sim G \sim A \supset \sim L \sim A$	RMP (1, 2)
4. $FA \supset MA$	Def. F/G, Def. M/L

T29. $LA \supset MA$

Proof:

1. $LA \supset GA$	A19
2. $GA \supset FA$	A11

3. $LA \supset FA$	SC2, RMP (1, 2)
4. $FA \supset MA$	T28
5. $LA \supset MA$	SC2, RMP (3, 4)

T30. $FLA \supset FA$

Proof:

1. $LA \supset GA$	A19
2. $GA \supset FA$	A11
3. $LA \supset FA$	SC2, RMP (1, 2)
4. $G(LA \supset FA)$	RG
5. $G(LA \supset FA) \supset (FLA \supset FFA)$	T1
6. $FLA \supset FFA$	RMP (4, 5)
7. $FFA \supset FA$	A8
8. $FLA \supset FA$	SC2, RMP (6, 7)

T31. $PLA \supset A$

Proof:

1. $LA \supset GA$	A19
2. $H(LA \supset GA)$	RH
3. $H(LA \supset GA) \supset (PLA \supset PGA)$	T2
4. $PLA \supset PGA$	RMP (2, 3)
5. $PGA \supset A$	T11
6. $PLA \supset A$	SC2, RMP (4, 5)

T32. $PLA \supset FA$

Proof:

1. $GA \supset FA$	A11
2. $GGA \supset GFA$	RG⊃
3. $FF{\sim}A \supset F{\sim}A$	A8
4. $(FF{\sim}A \supset F{\sim}A) \supset ({\sim}F{\sim}A \supset {\sim}FF{\sim}A)$	SC1
5. ${\sim}F{\sim}A \supset {\sim}FF{\sim}A$	RMP (3, 4)
6. $GA \supset GGA$	Def. F/G, SC15, REQ (5)
7. $GA \supset GFA$	SC2, RMP (2, 6)
8. $H(GA \supset GFA)$	RH
9. $H(GA \supset GFA) \supset (PGA \supset PGFA)$	T2
10. $PGA \supset PGFA$	SC2, RMP (8, 9)
11. $LA \supset GA$	A19

12. $H(LA \supset GA)$	RH
13. $H(LA \supset GA) \supset (PLA \supset PGA)$	T2
14. $PLA \supset PGA$	SC2, RMP (12, 13)
15. $PLA \supset PGFA$	SC2, RMP (14, 10)
16. $PGFA \supset FA$	T11
17. $PLA \supset FA$	SC2, RMP (15, 16)

T33. $PLA \supset LA$

Proof:

1. $MM{\sim}A \supset M{\sim}A$	A17
2. $(MM{\sim}A \supset M{\sim}A) \supset ({\sim}M{\sim}A \supset {\sim}MM{\sim}A)$	SC1
3. ${\sim}M{\sim}A \supset {\sim}MM{\sim}A$	SC2, RMP (1, 2)
4. $LA \supset LLA$	Def. M/L, REQ, SC15 (3)
5. $H(LA \supset LLA)$	RH
6. $H(LA \supset LLA) \supset (PLA \supset PLLA)$	T2
7. $PLA \supset PLLA$	RMP (5, 6)
8. $PLLA \supset LA$	T31
9. $PLA \supset LA$	SC2, RMP (7, 8)

T34. $PA \supset LPA$, where A contains no occurrences of F

Proof: Let A contain no occurrences of F

1. $A \supset LPA$	A20
2. $H(A \supset LPA)$	RH
3. $H(A \supset LPA) \supset (PA \supset PLPA)$	T2
4. $PA \supset PLPA$	RMP (2, 3)
5. $PLPA \supset LPA$	T33
6. $PA \supset LPA$	RMP (4, 5)

Incorporating the concept of a *prima facie* future into the semantic account of *OT* calls for several changes to our concept of an historical moment. An *OT*-historical moment is a quintuple of the sort $\langle \Omega, \mathbf{R}, \mathbf{B}, \varphi, R^{\varphi} \rangle$, the terms of which are as follows:

(i) Ω is (as usual) the set of truth-value assignments for *OT* indexed with integers,

(ii) $\mathbf{R}$ is a binary relation on the membership of Ω with the properties P1 (transitivity), P3 (left-linearity), P4, and P5 (non-endingness in the past and future),

(iii)   **B** is the set of all of the *linear* sub-relations of **R** (i.e., all the sub-relations of **R** having P1, P2, P3, P4, and P5),[11]

(iv) φ is an elemnt of Ω, and

(v) R^φ is a member of **B** which *passes through* φ (i.e., such that $(\exists x) R^\varphi(\varphi, x)$).

R is simply the extended (by P4 and P5) tree-like relation earlier discussed in connection with the semantics of K_b, and **B** is the set of all of its branches. At each member of Ω, in this case φ, one member of **B** is singled out, in this case the relation called R^φ. Obviously, for R^φ to serve as the *prima facie* future of φ, it must pass through φ, hence the restriction found in clause (v) above.

Proceeding, then, to the definitions of truth and validity for the statements of *OT*, take a statement *A* to be *true* at an *OT*-historical moment $\langle \Omega, \mathbf{R}, \mathbf{B}, \varphi, R^\varphi \rangle$ if:

(a) *A* is a statement letter, $\varphi(A) = 1$;

(b) *A* is of the sort $\sim B$, *B* is not true at $\langle \Omega, \mathbf{R}, \mathbf{B}, \varphi, R^\varphi \rangle$;

(c) *A* is of the sort $B \supset C$, either *B* is not true at $\langle \Omega, \mathbf{R}, \mathbf{B}, \varphi, R^\varphi \rangle$ or *C* is;

(d) *A* is of the sort *FB*, *B* is true at some $\langle \Omega, \mathbf{R}, \mathbf{B}, \mu, R^\mu \rangle$ such that $R^\varphi(\varphi, \mu)$;

(e) *A* is of the sort *PB*, *B* is true at some $\langle \Omega, \mathbf{R}, \mathbf{B}, \mu, R^\mu \rangle$ such that $R^\mu = R^\varphi$ and $R^\mu(\mu, \varphi)$; and

(f) *A* is of the sort *MB*, *B* is true at some $\langle \Omega, \mathbf{R}, \mathbf{B}, \mu, R^\mu \rangle$ such that $\mathbf{R}(\varphi, \mu)$.

Some explanation is required for clause (e). The stipulation $R^\mu = R^\varphi$ insures that if μ is in the past of φ (i.e., if $R^\varphi(\mu, \varphi)$), then φ lies on the *prima facie* future of μ (hence $R^\mu(\mu, \varphi)$). Note the concept of a *prima facie* future only has point for states of the world (members of Ω) which are either present or future. For a state of the world which is already past, the actual course of world-states serves as its future insofar as it actually *has* a future.

The other semantic notions — validity, satisfiability, and entailment — are defined for *OT* in the standard manner.

The reader may have wondered at the restriction placed on A20, and, by rebound, on T34. The point is best illustrated by exploring the situation which would obtain if no such restriction were imposed. The general thesis expressed by an unrestricted version of A20 is:

If *A is* the case, then it will necessarily be that *A was* the case.

This sounds innocuous enough – indeed, even desirable, given our view of temporal modality – but a danger lurks. For suppose *A* were of the sort *FB*. Then we would have:

FB ⊃ LPFB.

But a counter-example is easy to produce to the validity of this statement. For example, consider the below diagram.

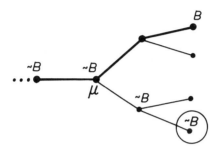

Suppose the uppermost branch is the *prima facie* future of the origin μ. Then indeed *FB* is true at μ, since *B* lies on its prima facie future. But, on the lower branches, e.g., at the node which is circled, *PFB* is *not* true. Hence, *LPFB* is not true at μ.

Such anomalous cases will not occur so long as *A* in *A ⊃ LPA* meets the restriction of A20 and is not a future tensed statement.

NOTES

[1] See Prior, 1967, Appendix A.

[2] Rescher and Urquhart, 1971, Chapter 4.

[3] Specifically, as in the Special Theory of Relativity. On this point see Rennie, 1969 and Lucas, 1971.

[4] A more detailed interpretation of K_b along these lines is found in Rescher and Urquhart, 1971, Chapter 4.

[5] This observation is Prior's. See Prior, 1967, p. 133.

[6] The standard work on Stoic logic is Mates, 1952. These definitions are Prior's.

[7] Although I have reproduced Prior's findings on the question, recent developments suggest that at least one of the entries in this table is incorrect. Rescher and Urquhart report that the Aristotelian fragment of *CR* and K_b is somewhat stronger than *B*, but is not S_5. They leave the nature of the system an open question.

[8] See Prior, 1967, Chapter 7, especially pp. 122–127. In addition Thomason, 1970a bears on the semantic formulation here given for *OT*. Also consult Vaughn McKim and Charles Davis, 'Temporal Modalities and the Future', *Notre Dame Journal of Formal Logic* (April 1976), pp. 233–238.

[9] '*O*' for Ockham, whose views on future contingency inspired this approach. Also see McArthur, 1975.

[10] These are often called *maximal R-chains in* Ω.

[11] A similar distinction between 'pure' future statements (for which A20 does not hold) and others (for which it does) is made by Ockham. See McArthur, 1975.

CHAPTER 4

QUANTIFICATIONAL TENSE LOGICS

4.1. THE Q-SYSTEMS

In this section and the next we shall investigate tense logics which are based on quantificational logics. The first of these bases, called Q, is the classical theory of quantification. The others, Q^* and Q^{**}, are *free* quantification theories which permit some of the individual constants (= free individual variables) to be non-designating.[1]

We shall begin by discussing the syntactical aspect of QK_t, the Q extension of K_t (see Section 2.1). Since all other quantificational tense logics have a similar syntactical formulation, we shall treat QK_t in some detail.

The primitive signs of QK_t are the following:

(i) the *individual variables*: x, y, z, x', y', etc.;[2]

(ii) the *individual constants*: a_1, a_2, a_3, etc.;

(iii) for each m from 0 on, the m-place *predicates*: $f_1^0, f_2^0, \ldots, f_1^1, f_2^1, \ldots,$ etc.;[3]

(iv) the *connectives*: $\sim$ and $\supset$;

(v) the *universal quantifier* $\forall$;

(vi) the *tense operators* F and P; and

(vii) left and right parentheses and the comma as *punctuations*.

As before, a *formula* of QK_t is any (finite) concatenation of signs of QK_t. Where A, B, and C are formulas, we shall take a *statement* of QK_t to be any formula of one of the following six sorts:

(i) $F^m(C_1, C_2, \ldots, C_m)$, where F^m is, for some m from 0 on, an m-place predicate, and $C_1, C_2, \ldots, C_m$ are (not necessarily distinct) individual constants;

(ii) $\sim A$, where A is a statement;

(iii) $(A \supset B)$, where A and B are statements;

(iv) $(\forall X)A(X/C)$, where X is an individual variable foreign to A, C is an individual constant, $A(X/C)$ is the result of replacing every occurrence of C in A by X, and A is a statement;

(v) FA, where A is a statement; and

(vi) PA, where A is a statement.

Statements of the first sort shall be called *atomic*.

The statement letters of previous chapters now occur as 0-place predicates, and they still are considered atomic statements. But, as clause (i) indicates, any m-place predicate (now with $m > 0$) followed by m individual constants also counts as an atomic statement. To illustrate, all three of the following are atomic statements of QK_t: f_1^0, $f_2^1(a_1)$, and $f_3^4(a_1, a_1, a_2, a_3)$. The superscript indicates the places of the predicate and the subscript serves to individuate it from others of the same number of places. The reader's attention is also called to clause (iv). The complicated phrasing of this clause is a product of the desire to prohibit any statement from having overlapping quantifiers to the same individual variable. Thus, by clause (iv), $(\forall x)(f_1^1(x) \supset (\forall x)f_2^1(x))$ *does not* count as a statement of QK_t. Clause (iv) does permit, however, *vacuous* quantifications, e.g., $(\forall x)(f_1^0 \supset f_1^0)$, to be statements.

From here on we shall use the notation $A(I/I')$, where I and I' are individual variables or constants, to indicate the result of replacing every occurrence of I' in A by I. Furthermore, A, B, and C shall be reserved to stand for either statements or *quasi-statements* of QK_t. Such quasi-statements are formulas of the sort $A(X/C)$, where A is a statement. Thus $f_1^1(x)$ is a quasi-statement as are $(\forall x)(f_2^1(x) \supset f_1^1(y))$ and $(\forall y)f_1^2(x, y)$. Since a statement need not contain an occurrence of an individual constant, our definition also includes statements as quasi-statements. Finally, in addition to X, Y and Z shall be used as syntactical variables for individual variables.

Our defined connectives and tense operators will be the same as in previous chapters, i.e. &, $\vee$, $\equiv$, G, and H. One more defined sign is useful in quantificational contexts, however, namely the dual of the universal quantifier. This sign is $\exists$ (the existential quantifier) and it is defined as follows.

$$(\exists X)A =_{df} \sim(\forall X)\sim A$$

As in previous accounts, where A is any statement or quasi-statement, $MI(A)$ shall denote the *mirror image* of A.

Our interest in this section, and in the sections which follow, lies not (for a change!) in the tense operators and the axioms which govern them, but rather in the quantificational aspect of QK_t and its extensions. Hence we spell out in full detail the axioms which make up the quantificational basis of QK_t. In place of K_t's axiom A1 (A, where A is a tautology), QK_t will have four axioms, borrowed from QC, the classical quantificational calculus. These axioms, as usual expressed as schemata, are as below.

Q1. $(\forall X)(A \supset B) \supset ((\forall X)A \supset (\forall X)B)$

Q2. $A \supset (\forall X)A$

Q3. $(\forall X)A \supset A(C/X)$, for any individual constant C

Q4. $(\forall X)A$, where, for some individual constant C foreign to $(\forall X)A$, $A(C/X)$ is an axiom.

Several comments on these axioms are in order here. First, Q2, although appearing quite strange, says nothing amiss. A, in its first occurrence, *must* be a statement, hence, by dint of clause (iv) of the rules of statementhood, X must be foreign to A. So $(\forall X)A$ is sure to be a vacuous quantification. Second, Q3, sometimes called the *axiom of specification*, permits the substitution of *any* individual constant for the variable of quantification. This is in line with our usual understanding of universal quantification, which will be spelled out when we turn to the semantics of QK_t. And, third, Q4, which replaces the more customary *rule of generalization*, permits the converse of Q3, only when $A(C/X)$ is itself an axiom. It is easily shown that the standard generalization *rule*:

If $\vdash A(C/X)$, then $\vdash (\forall X)A$, where C is foreign to A

is obtainable as a derived rule of QK_t. Putting the matter as in Q4 makes for a simpler meta-theory.[4] Note too, that this device has been used in an analogous manner in the statement of axioms A6 (GA, where A is an axiom) and A7 (HA, where A is an axiom).

Hence, our axiomatization of QK_t is as follows:

(1) Axiom schemata for QK_t

Q1–Q4

A2–A7 (K_t)

(2) Rule of Inference

      RMP

The usual definitions of proof, provability, theoremhood, and consistency carry over here from K_t. The five extra rules of inference are also available for use in QK_t. Because of the style of axiomatization we have utilized, their proofs for QK_t are identical to those on pp. 19–20.

To simplify proof of some of the theorems of QK_t, we will add one more rule of inference to those introduced in Chapter 2.

R∀.   If $\vdash A \supset B$, then $\vdash A \supset (\forall X)B(X/C)$, so long as X is foreign to A and C is foreign to $A \supset (\forall X)B$.

In addition to T1–T12 (the theorems of K_t), the theorems of QK_t include the following.

T35. $(\forall X)GA \supset G(\forall X)A$

Proof:

1. $(\forall X)GA \supset GA(C/X)$	Q3
2. $H((\forall X)GA \supset GA(C/X))$	RH
3. $H((\forall X)GA \supset GA(C/X)) \supset (P(\forall X)GA \supset PGA(C/X))$	T2
4. $P(\forall X)GA \supset PGA(C/X)$	RMP (2, 3)
5. $PGA(C/X) \supset A(C/X)$	T11
6. $P(\forall X)GA \supset A(C/X)$	SC2, RMP (4, 5)
7. $P(\forall X)GA \supset (\forall X)A$	R∀ (6)
8. $GP(\forall X)GA \supset G(\forall X)A$	RG⊃ (7)
9. $(\forall X)GA \supset GP(\forall X)GA$	A5
10. $(\forall X)GA \supset G(\forall X)A$	SC2, RMP (8, 9)

T36. $(\forall X)HA \supset H(\forall X)A$

Proof: By T35 and RMI.

T37. $G(\forall X)A \supset (\forall X)GA$

Proof:

1. $(\forall X)A \supset A(C/X)$	Q3
2. $G(\forall X)A \supset GA(C/X)$	RG⊃ (1)
3. $G(\forall X)A \supset (\forall X)GA$	R∀ (2)

T38. $H(\forall X)A \supset (\forall X)HA$

Proof: By T37 and RMI.

T39. $F(\forall X)A \supset (\forall X)FA$

Proof:

1. $(\forall X)A \supset A(C/X)$	Q3
2. $G((\forall X)A \supset A(C/X))$	RG
3. $G((\forall X)A \supset A(C/X)) \supset (F(\forall X)A \supset FA(C/X))$	T1

4. $F(\forall X)A \supset FA(C/X)$ RMP $(2, 3)$
5. $F(\forall X)A \supset (\forall X)FA$ R$\forall$ (4)

T40. $P(\forall X)A \supset (\forall X)PA$

Proof: By T39 and RMI.

T41. $F(\exists X)A \supset (\exists X)FA$

Proof:
1. $(\forall X)G{\sim}A \supset G(\forall X){\sim}A$ T35
2. $((\forall X)G{\sim}A \supset G(\forall X){\sim}A) \supset ({\sim}G(\forall X){\sim}A \supset$
   $\qquad {\sim}(\forall X)G{\sim}A)$ SC1
3. ${\sim}G(\forall X){\sim}A \supset {\sim}(\forall X)G{\sim}A$ RMP $(1, 2)$
4. $F{\sim}(\forall X){\sim}A \supset {\sim}(\forall X){\sim}FA$ Def. F/G, SC15, REQ
5. $F(\exists X)A \supset (\exists X)FA$ Def. $\exists$ / $\forall$

T42. $P(\exists X)A \supset (\exists X)PA$

Proof: By T41 and RMI.

T43. $(\exists X)FA \supset F(\exists X)A$

Proof:
1. $G(\forall X){\sim}A \supset (\forall X)G{\sim}A$ T37
2. $(G(\forall X){\sim}A \supset (\forall X)G{\sim}A) \supset ({\sim}(\forall X)G{\sim}A \supset$
   $\qquad {\sim}G(\forall X){\sim}A)$ SC1
3. ${\sim}(\forall X)G{\sim}A \supset {\sim}G(\forall X){\sim}A$ RMP $(1, 2)$
4. ${\sim}(\forall X){\sim}FA \supset F{\sim}(\forall X){\sim}A$ Def. F/G, SC15, REQ
5. $(\exists X)FA \supset F(\exists X)A$ Def. $\exists$ / $\forall$

T44. $(\exists X)PA \supset P(\exists X)A$

Proof: By T43 and RMI.

All of these 'mixing' theorems are variants of what is sometimes called the *Barcan Formula* in modal logics. Since there is no general agreement on terminology in the case of tense logic, we feel free to dub T35 as the *Future Barcan Theorem*, T36 as the *Past Barcan Theorem*, T37 as the *Converse Future Barcan Theorem*, and T38 as the *Converse Past Barcan Theorem*.

Passing next to the semantics of QK_t, we shall again utilize historical moments of the sort $\langle \Omega, R, \varphi \rangle$, where $\Omega, R,$ and φ are defined as they were in Chapter 2. Note, however, that the (indexed) truth-value assignments which make up Ω are now to *all atomic statements of QK_t*. Thus the members of Ω assign truth-values to infinitely many more atomic statements than the truth-value assignments did in K_t.

Truth is defined for the statements of QK_t as follows. A statement A is *true* at $\langle \Omega, R, \varphi \rangle$ if:

(i) A is atomic, $\varphi(A) = 1$;

(ii) A is of the sort $\sim B$, B is not true at $\langle \Omega, R, \varphi \rangle$;

(iii) A is of the sort $B \supset C$, either B is not true at $\langle \Omega, R, \varphi \rangle$ or C is;

(iv) A is of the sort $(\forall X)B$, $B(C/X)$ is true at $\langle \Omega, R, \varphi \rangle$ for *every* individual constant C of QK_t;

(v) A is of the sort FB, B is true at some $\langle \Omega, R, \mu \rangle$ such that $R(\varphi, \mu)$; and

(vi) A is of the sort PB, B is true at some $\langle \Omega, R, \mu \rangle$ such that $R(\mu, \varphi)$.

Although any set of statements of QK_t which are all true at some QK_t-historical moment is sure to be *satisfiable*, the converse is not the case. So care must be taken in the definition of satisfiability in QK_t. The primary difficulty arises over infinite sets of statements. Consider, for example, the following set:

$$\{f_1^1(a_1), f_1^1(a_2), f_1^1(a_3), \ldots, \sim(\forall x)f_1^1(x)\}.$$

There surely is no QK_t-historical moment at which all the members of this set are true.[5] So, if we were to define satisfaction in the usual manner (i.e., a set is satisfiable if all the members are true at some historical moment), we would have to declare this set not to be satisfiable. But, it is easy to show that if a set of statements $\{A_1, A_2, \ldots, \sim B\}$ is not satisfiable, then the set $\{A_1, A_2, \ldots\}$ entails B. Hence we would have to admit that in QK_t,

$$\{f_1^1(a_1), f_1^1(a_2), f_1^1(a_3), \ldots\} \text{ entails } (\forall x)f_1^1(x).$$

However, given our axiomatization of QK_t, $(\forall x)f_1^1(x)$ is *not* provable from $\{f_1^1(a_1), f_1^1(a_2), f_1^1(a_3), \ldots\}$. And our account of QK_t would not provide the exact correspondance between the deductive presentation and the semantic presentation which is so desirable.

The literature on substitutional semantics for quantificational logics contains several ploys for skirting this problem. Of these, we prefer the following. Since the example discussed above depends upon there being an infinite number of individual constants which occur in the membership of the set, we have only to worry about sets of this sort. All others, to which an infinite number of individual constants are foreign, pose no difficulty. We shall call sets of this type *infinitely extendible*, and those of the former type *non-infinitely extendible*. It is important to realize that many infinite sets of statements *are* infinitely extendible. For example, the set $\{f_1^1(a_2), f_1^1(a_4), f_1^1(a_6),$ ...$\}$, although infinite, has infinitely many individual constants of QK_t foreign to it. This realization provides the key to our solution.

First, any set whose members are all true on some historical moment will be called *verifiable* in QK_t. Next, where S is a non-infinitely extendible set, E_S is the set of all the individual constants which occur in the members of S, and Φ is a one-to-one mapping of E_S onto the set of all of the individual constants of QK_t, we shall take the Φ-*image* — denoted by $\Phi(A)$ — of a member A of S to be as follows:

(i) A itself, in case no individual constants occur in A, or

(ii) in case individual constants $C_1, C_2, \ldots, C_m$ ($m \geq 1$) occur in A, then, where $\Phi(C_i)$ ($1 \leq i \leq m$) denotes the value of Φ at C_i, $A(\Phi(C_1), \Phi(C_2), \ldots, \Phi(C_m)/C_1, C_2, \ldots, C_m)$.

The Φ-image of the set S — denoted by $\Phi(S)$ — shall be the set of the Φ-images of the members of S.

For any two sets S and S' of statements of QK_t, if E_S is defined as above for S, then we shall say that S *is isomorphic to* S' if S' is $\Phi(S)$ for some one-to-one mapping Φ of E_S onto the set of the individual constants of QK_t.

Turning then to the definition of satisfiability in QK_t, we shall take a set S to be *satisfiable in* QK_t if either:

(i) S is verifiable, or

(ii) S is isomorphic to a set S' which is verifiable.

To illustrate the point, consider S to be $\{f_1^1(a_1), f_1^1(a_2), f_1^1(a_3), \ldots, \sim(\forall x)f_1^1(x)\}$, E_S to consist of all the individual constants of QK_t, and Φ to be a one-to-one mapping from the set of individual constants of QK_t to the set of individual constants of QK_t having *even* indices, such that $\Phi(a_i)$ is a_{2i}. Then S' would be $\{f_1^1(a_2), f_1^1(a_4), f_1^1(a_6), \ldots, \sim(\forall x)f_1^1(x)\}$. Note that S' is indeed verifiable at any historical moment $\langle \Omega, R, \varphi \rangle$ such that each of $f_1^1(a_2)$, $f_1^1(a_4), f_1^1(a_6), \ldots$ is true at $\langle \Omega, R, \varphi \rangle$ and some other statement $f_1^1(a_i)$, say $f_1^1(a_1)$, is false. Furthermore, S is isomorphic to S'. Hence, our original set S is satisfiable in QK_t.

As for validity and entailment, they are defined as before: a statement A is *valid* in QK_t if A is true at every historical moment of QK_t, and a set S *entails* a statement A in QK_t if $S \cup \{\sim A\}$ is not satisfiable in QK_t.

The details of our semantic account of QK_t will perhaps be clearer if several of the theorems are shown to be QK_t-valid.

T35. $(\forall X)GA \supset G(\forall X)A$ (Future Barcan Theorem)

Suppose $(\forall X)GA$ is true at $\langle \Omega, R, \varphi \rangle$. Then for every individual constant C of QK_t, $GA(C/X)$ is sure to be true at $\langle \Omega, R, \varphi \rangle$. Hence, for every $\langle \Omega, R, \mu \rangle$ such that $R(\varphi, \mu)$, $A(C/X)$ will be true at $\langle \Omega, R, \mu \rangle$, for every constant C. Hence, $(\forall X)A$ is true at every $\langle \Omega, R, \mu \rangle$ such that $R(\varphi, \mu)$, hence $G(\forall X)A$ is true at $\langle \Omega, R, \varphi \rangle$. Hence, whenever $(\forall X)GA$ is true at an historical moment, so is $G(\forall X)A$. Hence, T35 is valid in QK_t.

T37. $G(\forall X)A \supset (\forall X)GA$ (Converse Future Barcan Theorem)

Suppose $G(\forall X)A$ is true at $\langle \Omega, R, \varphi \rangle$. Then, at every $\langle \Omega, R, \mu \rangle$ such that $R(\varphi, \mu)$, $(\forall X)A$ is true at $\langle \Omega, R, \mu \rangle$. Hence, $A(C/X)$ is true at (every) $\langle \Omega, R, \mu \rangle$, for every individual constant C. Hence, for every individual constant C, $GA(C/X)$ is true at $\langle \Omega, R, \varphi \rangle$. Hence, $(\forall X)GA$ is true at $\langle \Omega, R, \varphi \rangle$. Hence, whenever $G(\forall X)A$ is true at an historical moment, so is $(\forall X)GA$. Hence, T37 is valid in QK_t.

It is easy to see that the validity of T35 and T37 depend on *every* individual constant of QK_t figuring in the computation of the truth of quantificational statements at all of the historical moments. Two other quantificational bases for tense logics will be discussed in the next section which lack this feature – they permit individual constants to be non-designating at some historical moments and designating at others.

Though it is not at issue here, the other tense logics of Chapters 2 and 3 can be extended into Q systems by replacing A1 with Q1–Q4, and utilizing the syntax and semantics, *mutatis mutandis*, of QK_t. This results in QCR, QK_b, QCL, and so forth.

4.2 THE Q^* AND Q^{**} SYSTEMS

The Q^* systems of tense logic, to be known as QK_t^*, QCR^*, etc., differ syntactically from the Q systems in only one respect. To be specific, they replace axiom Q3 (the axiom of specification) with two other axioms. These are:

Q3*a. $(\forall Y)((\forall X)A \supset A(Y/X))$

Q3*b. $(\forall Y)(\forall X)A \supset (\forall X)(\forall Y)A$

Hence, QK_t^* is axiomatized as follows.[6]
(1) Axiom Schemata for QK_t^*

Q1–Q2

Q3*a–Q3*b

Q4

A2–A7

(2) Rule of Inference

RMP

The net effect of this change in axioms is to block the deductive relationship between universal quantifications and their substitution instances. Hence Q3 (i.e., $(\forall X)A \supset A(C/X)$) is *not* a theorem for any Q^* system.

A glance at the proofs given in Section 4.1 for theorems T35–T39 will reveal that the lack of Q3 effectively eliminates these statements from theoremhood in QK_t^*. Hence the sets

$$\{G(\forall X)A, (\exists X)F{\sim}A\}$$
$$\{(\forall X)GA, F{\sim}(\forall X)A\}$$

are consistent in QK_t^*.

As suggested in Chapter 1, the semantic treatment of the Q^* systems makes the point of the replacement of axiom Q3 by Q3*a and Q3*b somewhat clearer. In the Q systems, a universal quantification was certified as true at an historical moment if *every* substitution instance was true at that moment. Here, however, only some of the substitution instances come into play. Formally, we shall pair a set of individual constants with each (indexed) truth-value assignment. And it shall be the individual constants in these sets which determine which substitution instances are relevant to the truth of a universal quantification in QK_t^*.

The members of Ω are, consequently, pairs of the sort $\langle \varphi, E \rangle$, where φ is a truth-value assignment and E is a set (possibly empty) of individual constants of QK_t^*. E shall be called φ's *designating set*. R, as usual, is a dyadic relation on the members of Ω.

So, take a statement A to be *true* at a QK_t^*-historical moment $\langle \Omega, R, \langle \varphi, E \rangle \rangle$ if:

(i) A is of one of the sorts $F^m(C_1, C_2, \ldots, C_m), {\sim}B, B \supset C, FB$, and PB, A is true on the same conditions as in QK_t, and

(ii) A is of the sort $(\forall X)B, B(C/X)$ is true at $\langle \Omega, R, \langle \varphi, E \rangle \rangle$ for *every* C in E.

An immediate consequence of clause (ii) is the automatic truth of every universal quantification when the designation set E is empty at an historical moment. This also insures that the negation of every universal quantification is false, and, hence, that every existential quantification is false as well.

The definitions of satisfiability, validity, and entailment for QK_t^* are as for QK_t.

On this semantics, each historical moment may have a unique set of individual constants which are taken as designating at that moment. So the quantifier, of any statement true at that moment, ranges over only those individual constants which designate. This gives a definite temporal flavor to the quantifiers which they lack in the Q systems. Thus, in the Q^* systems it is appropriate to read $\forall x$ as 'For every X at the present' and $\exists X$ as 'There exists an X at the present such that'.

How our semantics for QK_t^* blocks the validity of ordinary specification and the Barcan Theorems is illustrated by the following counter-examples.

(1) $(\forall X)A \supset A(C/X)$

Let $\langle \Omega, R, \langle \varphi, E \rangle \rangle$ be such that $E = \{a_1, a_2\}$. Then if both $A(a_1/X)$ and $A(a_2/X)$ are true at $\langle \Omega, R, \langle \varphi, E \rangle \rangle$, so is $(\forall X)A$. But, suppose $A(a_3/X)$ is *false* at $\langle \Omega, R, \langle \varphi, E \rangle \rangle$. Then so is the conditional $(\forall X)A \supset A(a_3/X)$, and, hence, $(\forall X)A \supset A(C/X)$ is not QK_t^*-valid.

(2) $(\forall X)GA \supset G(\forall X)A$

Suppose $E = \emptyset$ at $\langle \Omega, R, \langle \varphi, E \rangle \rangle$. Then $(\forall X)GA$ is true at $\langle \Omega, R, \langle \varphi, E \rangle \rangle$. However, at some $\langle \Omega, R, \langle \mu, E' \rangle \rangle$ such that $R(\langle \varphi, E \rangle, \langle \mu, E' \rangle)$, let some instance $A(C/X)$ of $(\forall X)A$ be false, where C is a member of E'. Then $(\forall X)A$ is false at $\langle \Omega, R, \langle \mu, E' \rangle \rangle$, and $G(\forall X)A$ is false at $\langle \Omega, R, \langle \varphi, E \rangle \rangle$. Hence the conditional $(\forall X)GA \supset G(\forall X)A$ is false at $\langle \Omega, R, \langle \varphi, E \rangle \rangle$, and is not QK_t^*-valid.

(3) $H(\forall X)A \supset (\forall X)HA$

Suppose $(\forall X)A$ is true at every $\langle \Omega, R, \langle \mu, E' \rangle \rangle$ such that $R(\langle \mu, E' \rangle, \langle \varphi, E \rangle)$. Then $H(\forall X)A$ is true at $\langle \Omega, R, \langle \varphi, E \rangle \rangle$. Further suppose that for *some* $\langle \Omega, R, \langle \mu, E' \rangle \rangle$, E' is a proper subset of E. Then, let C be an individual constant belonging to E but not to E' such that $A(C/X)$ is false at $\langle \Omega, R, \langle \mu, E' \rangle \rangle$. Then $HA(C/X)$ is false at $\langle \Omega, R, \langle \varphi, E \rangle \rangle$ for some C in E. Hence $(\forall X)HA$ is false at $\langle \Omega, R, \langle \varphi, E \rangle \rangle$, and so is the conditional $H(\forall X)A \supset (\forall X)HA$. Hence, $H(\forall X)A \supset (\forall X)HA$ is not QK_t^*-valid.

Similar counter-examples to the remaining Barcan Theorems of Section 4.1 are easily constructed along the same lines as those above. And this holds as well for all of the extensions of $QK\uparrow$.

Yet another quantificational basis is available for tense logics which retains as valid the Converse Barcan Theorems, T37 and T38, but not the others. Systems utilizing this basis we call $Q**$ systems, e.g., $QK\uparrow^{**}$, QCR^{**}, etc.

$QK\uparrow^{**}$ is an extension of the quantificational basis of $QK\uparrow$, which adds a restricted form of Q3 plus T37 and T38 as axioms.

(1) Axiom Schemata for $QK\uparrow^{**}$

Q1–Q2

Q3*a–Q3*b

Q4

Q5. $(\forall X)A \supset A(C/X)$, where A contains *no tense operators*

A2–A7

T37. $G(\forall X)A \supset (\forall X)GA$

T38. $H(\forall X)A \supset (\forall X)HA$

(2) Rule of Inference

RMP

The reappearance of the specification axiom, Q5, in this restricted form does not permit proof of T35 (the Future Barcan Theorem) or T37 (the Past Barcan Theorem). The proofs of these require $(\forall X)GA \supset GA(C/X)$ or $(\forall X)HA \supset HA(C/X)$, respectively, which are both not instances of axiom Q5.[7]

The remainder of the syntactical account of $QK\uparrow^{**}$ follows that of $QK\uparrow$.

The $QK\uparrow^{**}$-historical moments are somewhat more complicated those for $QK\uparrow$. Here we will utilize *partial* truth-value assignments, and allow some atomic statements to go truth-valueless, or, as we shall say, *unvalued*, on a truth-value assignment. The key factors in these partial assignments are the sets of designating individual constants we first introduced in our semantic account of $QK\uparrow$. The formal details are as follows. The set of all atomic statements of $QK\uparrow^{**}$ shall be sorted into disjoint (i.e., non-overlapping) sets: S_C, having as members all atomic statements containing individual constants, and S_{NC}, having as members all atomic statements containing no individual constants (i.e., all 0-place predicates of QK_t^{**}). Where E is a (possible empty) set of individual constants, let S_C^E be the subset of S_C to which belong all atomic statements containing *only* individual constants in E. Then, understand by a truth-value assignment φ for QK_t^{**} *relative to a set E of individual constants* any function from the union of S_{NC} and S_C^E to $\{1, 0\}$. Atomic statements receiving either 1 or 0 by such an assignment are said to be *valued* by the assignment, others are said to be *unvalued*. Note that if an atomic statement A contains an individual constant which is not a member of E, then A is sure to be unvalued by any assignment made relative to E.

Where φ is a truth-value assignment relative to E, and E is a set of individual constants, the pair $\langle \varphi, E \rangle$ shall be called a *truth-pair*. Ω, in the historical moments of QK_t^{**}, shall be a set of such truth-pairs, and R, as usual, any dyadic relation on the members of Ω. (Once again, to insure that a given partial truth-value assignment can occur more than once in Ω, we assume all assignments to be indexed.)

Our conditions for the truth of a statement A reflect that in some cases A will not have a value at an QK_t^{**}-historical moment. So we spell out the various possibilities in detail.

At the QK_t^{**}-historical moment $\langle \Omega, R, \langle \varphi, E \rangle \rangle$:

(i) If A is atomic, then
   a. A is true if $\varphi(A) = 1$,
   b. A is false if $\varphi(A) = 0$, and
   c. A is unvalued otherwise.

(ii) If A is of the sort $\sim B$, then
   a. A is true if B is false,
   b. A is false if B is true, and
   c. A is unvalued if B is.

(iii) If A is of the sort $B \supset C$, then
   a. A is true if either B is false and C is true or false, or B is true and C is true,
   b. A is false if B is true and C is false, and
   c. A is unvalued if either B or C is unvalued.[8]

(iv) If A is of the sort $(\forall X)B$, then
   a. A is true if $B(C/X)$ is true for every C in E,
   b. A is false if some $B(C/X)$ is false, where C is a member of E, and every other $B(C/X)$ such that C is a member of E is either true or false, and

c. A is unvalued if any $B(C/X)$ such that C is a member of E is unvalued.

(v) If A is of the sort FB, then

a. A is true if B is true at some $\langle \Omega, R, \langle \mu, E' \rangle \rangle$ such that $R(\langle \varphi, E \rangle, \langle \mu, E' \rangle)$, and B is either true or false at every $\langle \Omega, R, \langle \mu, E' \rangle \rangle$ such that $R(\langle \varphi, E \rangle, \langle \mu, E' \rangle)$,

b. A is false if B is false at every $\langle \Omega, R, \langle \mu, E' \rangle \rangle$ such that $R(\langle \varphi, E \rangle, \langle \mu, E' \rangle)$, and

c. A is unvalued if B is unvalued at some $\langle \Omega, R, \langle \mu, E' \rangle \rangle$ such that $R(\langle \varphi, E \rangle, \langle \mu, E' \rangle)$.

(vi) If A is of the sort PB, then

a. A is true if B is true at some $\langle \Omega, R, \langle \mu, E' \rangle \rangle$ such that $R(\langle \mu, E' \rangle, \langle \varphi, E \rangle)$, and B is either true or false at every $\langle \Omega, R, \langle \mu, E' \rangle \rangle$ such that $R(\langle \mu, E' \rangle, \langle \varphi, E \rangle)$,

b. A is false if B is false at every $\langle \Omega, R, \langle \mu, E' \rangle \rangle$ such that $R(\langle \mu, E' \rangle, \langle \varphi, E \rangle)$, and

c. A is unvalued if B is unvalued at some $\langle \Omega, R, \langle \mu, E' \rangle \rangle$ such that $R(\langle \mu, E' \rangle, \langle \varphi, E \rangle)$.

Satisfiability and entailment are defined for QK_t^{**} in the same way as for QK_t^*. But we now take a statement to be QK_t^{**}-*valid* if it is true or unvalued at every QK_t^{**}-historical moment.

Appearances to the contrary, it turns out that the classical fragment of QK_t^{**}, i.e., all those statements which do not contain occurrences of tense operators, is exactly the classical fragment of the Q systems. Hence the extra complications in our semantic account of QK_t^{**} only affects statements containing tense operators, and, of course, quantifiers.

It remains to be shown that T37 and T38 are valid on this semantics and that counter-examples are still available for T35 and T36. By way of introduction, it should be pointed out that Q5 $-(\forall X)A \supset A(C/X)$, where A contains no tense operators $-$ is obviously valid in QK_t^{**} due to clause (iv) of our truth conditions. For suppose $A(C/X)$ were false at an historical moment $\langle \Omega, R, \langle \varphi, E \rangle \rangle$. Then C is sure to be a member of E. Hence $(\forall X)A$ is false as well. Thus when $(\forall X)A$ is true at $\langle \Omega, R, \langle \varphi, E \rangle \rangle$, $A(C/X)$ is sure to be true, if C is a member of E, or unvalued. So the conditional $(\forall X)A \supset A(C/X)$ (again presuming that no tense operators occur in A) is sure to be true or unvalued at $\langle \Omega, R, \langle \varphi, E \rangle \rangle$ for every individual constant C. Hence Q5 is valid in QK_t^{**}. On the other hand, when A contains a tense operator, counter-examples crop up. For suppose $(\forall X)A$ is of the sort $(\forall Y)FB$. Then at $\langle \Omega, R, \langle \varphi, E \rangle \rangle$, suppose $E = \emptyset$, making $(\forall Y)FB$ true. However, also suppose that $FB(C/Y)$ is false at every $\langle \Omega, R, \langle \mu, E' \rangle \rangle$ such that $R(\langle \varphi, E \rangle, \langle \mu, E' \rangle)$, for one or more individual constants. Then the conditional $(\forall Y)FB \supset FB(C/Y)$ is *not* true or unvalued at $\langle \Omega, R, \langle \varphi, E \rangle \rangle$ for every C. Hence it is not QK_t^{**}-valid.

T37. $G(\forall X)A \supset (\forall X)GA$

Suppose $G(\forall X)A$ is true at $\langle \Omega, R, \langle \varphi, E \rangle \rangle$. Then, for every $\langle \Omega, R, \langle \mu, E' \rangle \rangle$ such that $R(\langle \varphi, E \rangle, \langle \mu, E' \rangle)$, $(\forall X)A$ is true at $\langle \Omega, R, \langle \varphi, E \rangle \rangle$, and, for every C in E', $A(C/X)$ is true as well. Now, suppose $(\forall X)GA$ were false at $\langle \Omega, R, \langle \varphi, E \rangle \rangle$. Then $GA(C/X)$ would be false, for some C in E. Hence $A(C/X)$ would be false at $\langle \Omega, R, \langle \mu, E' \rangle \rangle$. But if $A(C/X)$ is false at $\langle \Omega, R, \langle \mu, E' \rangle \rangle$, C must be a member of E'. But this is impossible, so $(\forall X)GA$ cannot be false at $\langle \Omega, R, \langle \varphi, E \rangle \rangle$ if $G(\forall X)A$ is true. Hence T37 is either true or unvalued at $\langle \Omega, R, \langle \varphi, E \rangle \rangle$, and is valid in QK_t^{**}.

T38. $H(\forall X)A \supset (\forall X)HA$

By an argument similar to the one above, if $H(\forall X)A$ is true at $\langle \Omega, R, \langle \varphi, E \rangle \rangle$, then either $(\forall X)HA$ is also true or is unvalued. Hence, the conditional $H(\forall X)A \supset (\forall X)HA$ is either true or unvalued, and, hence, is QK_t^{**}-valid.

As far as counter-examples to T35 and T36 are concerned, the ones given on p. 62 will serve here as well. Hence neither is valid in QK_t^{**}.

NOTES

[1] More about free quantification theory can be had from Leblanc, 1976.

[2] Infinite stocks of individual variables, individual constants, and, for each m, m-place predicates are assumed here.

[3] 0-place predicates play the role of statement letters.

[4] See McArthur and Leblanc, 1975 for illustrations.

[5] But the set is satisfiable on model-theoretic semantics. For complete details on this matter see Leblanc, 1976.

[6] The Q-systems are based on those developed by Kripke (see Kripke, 1963) and Leblanc (see Leblanc, 1971) for quantificational modal logics. QCL^* is equivalent to the free, quantificational tense logic pioneered by Cocchiarella in 1966.

[7] Q3*a and Q3*b, as well as T37 and T38 are somewhat redundant as axioms of QK_t^{**}. They turn out to be provable with restrictions similar to that on Q5. However, given our semantics they are valid in their unrestricted forms and must be counted as axioms.

[8] These truth conditions are similar to those used by Hughes and Cresswell for their version of QS_t^*. Although they are not three-valued, they are similar to Bochvar's three-valued semantics for classical logic. See Rescher, 1969, pp. 29–34.

CHAPTER 5

SOUNDNESS AND COMPLETENESS THEOREMS
FOR TENSE LOGIC

The central task of this chapter is to show the Soundness and Completeness of our axiomatizations of the various tense logic systems. This amounts to showing that a statement A is provable (in a given system) from a set S of statements if and only if S entails A (in that system). The upshot of this result is the exact correspondence of the syntactical-deductive and the semantic accounts given for the system.

We will establish this correspondence for K_t in two theorems, after prefatory lemmas and sundry definitions. Afterwards, instructions will be supplied for extending the proofs to many of the other systems of tense logic.

Except at crucial points our proofs will be somewhat sketchy. The lines of argument, in many such cases, will be familiar from truth-functional logic.[1]

Our first two lemmas deal with various aspects of provability and consistency in K_t. (Note: from here on, we often leave off the 'in K_t' and just speak of consistency, provability, etc.)

LEMMA 1. (a) If A belongs to S, or is an axiom, then $S \vdash A$.

(b) If $S \vdash A$, there is a finite subset S' of S such that $S' \vdash A$.

(c) If $S \vdash A$, then $S \cup S' \vdash A$, for any set S'.

(d) If $S \vdash A$ and $S \vdash A \supset B$, then $S \vdash B$.

(e) If $S \cup \{A\} \vdash B$, then $S \vdash A \supset B$ (The Deduction Theorem).

(f) If $S \vdash A \supset B$, then $S \cup \{A\} \vdash B$.

Proof: (a)–(c) By the definition of a proof (see p. 18).

(d) The column made up of any proof of A from S, followed by any proof of $A \supset B$ from S, followed by B, constitutes a proof of B from S.

(e) Let the column made up of $C_1, C_2, \ldots, C_k \ (= B)$ constitute a proof of B from $S \cup \{A\}$. Then by mathematical induction on i, for each i from 1 through k, it is easily shown that $S \vdash A \supset C_i$ and, hence, in particular, that $S \vdash A \supset B$.

Base Case: $i = 1$. C_1 is either an axiom, in which case $S \vdash C_1$ by (a), or a member of S, in which case $S \vdash C_1$ also by (a). If C_1 is A, then since $A \supset A$ is an axiom (by A1), we have $S \vdash A \supset C_1$ by (d). Otherwise, since $C_1 \supset (A \supset C_1)$ is an axiom, we have $S \vdash A \supset C_1$ by (d) again.

Inductive Case: $i > 1$. Suppose for every C_g, where $g < i$, that $S \vdash A \supset C_g$. Then if C_i is either a member of S or an axiom, we have $S \vdash A \supset C_i$ by the above argument. So suppose C_i follows from two previous entries, say C_d and C_e ($= C_d \supset C_i$), by RMP. By the hypothesis of the induction, $S \vdash A \supset C_d$ and $S \vdash A \supset (C_d \supset C_i)$. Hence, since $(A \supset (C_d \supset C_i)) \supset ((A \supset C_d) \supset (A \supset C_i))$ is an axiom, it follows that $S \vdash A \supset C_i$ by (a) and (d).

Hence, in every case, $S \vdash A \supset C_i$, thus, $S \vdash A \supset B$.

(f) Let the column made up of $C_1, C_2, \ldots, C_k$ constitute a proof of $A \supset B$ from S. Then the column $C_1, C_2, \ldots, C_k, A, B$ constitutes a proof of B from $S \cup \{A\}$.

LEMMA 2. (a) If $S \vdash A$, then $S \cup \{\sim A\}$ is inconsistent.

(b) If $S \cup \{\sim A\}$ is inconsistent, then $S \vdash A$.

(c) If $S \vdash A$ and $S \vdash \sim A$, then S is inconsistent.

Proof:

(a) Both $A \supset ((p \supset p) \supset A)$ and $((p \supset p) \supset A) \supset (\sim A \supset \sim (p \supset p))$ are axioms by A1. So, by Lemma 1(a), $S \vdash A \supset ((p \supset p) \supset A)$. Hence, by Lemma 1(d), if $S \vdash A$ then $S \vdash (p \supset p) \supset A$. But, by Lemma 1(a) again, $S \vdash ((p \supset p) \supset (\sim A \supset \sim (p \supset p))$. Hence, by Lemma 1(d) again, $S \vdash \sim A \supset \sim (p \supset p)$. Hence, by Lemma 1(f), $S \cup \{\sim A\} \vdash \sim (p \supset p)$.

(b) Suppose $S \cup \{\sim A\} \vdash \sim (p \supset p)$. Hence, $S \vdash \sim A \supset \sim (p \supset p)$ by Lemma 1(e). But, by A1, $(\sim A \supset \sim (p \supset p)) \supset ((p \supset p) \supset A)$ is an axiom, and so $S \vdash (p \supset p) \supset A$, by Lemma 1 (a) and (d). But $S \vdash p \supset p$ by A1 and Lemma 1(a). Hence, by Lemma 1(d), $S \vdash A$.

(c) By the arguments in (a) above, if $S \vdash A$, then $S \vdash \sim A \supset \sim (p \supset p)$. Hence if $S \vdash \sim A$ as well, then $S \vdash \sim (p \supset p)$.

Our next two lemmas bear directly on the soundness of our axioms. They are followed by The Soundness Theorem.

LEMMA 3. If A is an axiom of K_t (i.e., of one of the sorts A1–A7), then A is K_t-valid.

Proof: (i) Suppose A is a tautology (A1). Then A is sure to be true at every K_t-historical moment by definition.

(ii) Suppose A is of the sort $G(B \supset C) \supset (GB \supset GC)$ (A2). Then as was shown on p. 23, A is K_t-valid.

(iii) Suppose A is of the sort $H(B \supset C) \supset (HB \supset HC)$ (A3). Then suppose $H(B \supset C)$ is true at $\langle \Omega, R, \varphi \rangle$. Hence, at every $\langle \Omega, R, \mu \rangle$ such that $R(\mu, \varphi)$, $B \supset C$ is sure to be true. Now suppose HB is true at $\langle \Omega, R, \varphi \rangle$. Then B is true at every $\langle \Omega, R, \mu \rangle$ such that $R(\mu, \varphi)$, and, thus, so is C. Hence HC is true at $\langle \Omega, R, \varphi \rangle$, as is the conditional $H(B \supset C) \supset (HB \supset HC)$. Thus A3 is K_t-valid.

(iv) Suppose A is of the sort $B \supset HFB$ (A4). Then suppose B is true at $\langle \Omega, R, \varphi \rangle$. *Case 1*: There is no μ such that $R(\mu, \varphi)$. Then HFB is sure to be true at $\langle \Omega, R, \varphi \rangle$. *Case 2*: Suppose there are μ's such that $R(\mu, \varphi)$. Then, at any such $\langle \Omega, R, \mu \rangle$, FB is sure to be true. Hence, HFB is sure to be true at $\langle \Omega, R, \varphi \rangle$. So, in either case, the conditional $B \supset HFB$ is true at $\langle \Omega, R, \varphi \rangle$, and, hence, is K_t-valid.

(v) Suppose A is of the sort $B \supset GPB$ (A5). Proof is left to the reader.

(vi) Suppose A is of the sort GB, where B is one of the five sorts A1–A5, or of the sort HB (A6–A7). Then B is sure to be true at every K_t-historical moment. In particular, at $\langle \Omega, R, \varphi \rangle$, B is sure to be true at every μ in Ω such that either $R(\mu, \varphi)$ or $R(\varphi, \mu)$.

Case 1: Suppose there are no μ's such that $R(\varphi, \mu)$. Then GB is true at $\langle \Omega, R, \varphi \rangle$.

Case 2: Suppose there are no μ's such that $R(\mu, \varphi)$. Then HB is true at $\langle \Omega, R, \varphi \rangle$.

Case 3: Suppose there are μ's such that $R(\varphi, \mu)$ and $R(\mu, \varphi)$. Then since B is true at every $\langle \Omega, R, \mu \rangle$, GB and HB are sure to be true at $\langle \Omega, R, \varphi \rangle$.

Hence, where B is an axiom of K_t, GB and HB are K_t-valid.

LEMMA 4. If S is inconsistent in K_t, then S is not satisfiable in K_t.

Proof: Let the column consisting of $C_1, C_2, \ldots, C_k$ ($= \sim(p \supset p)$) constitute a proof of $\sim(p \supset p)$ from S. Then suppose, for a reductio ad absurdum, that S is satisfiable. Then there is an historical moment $\langle \Omega, R, \varphi \rangle$ at which all the members of S are true. By mathematical induction on i, for each i from 1 through k, it is easy to show that if S is satisfiable, then each C_i is true at $\langle \Omega, R, \varphi \rangle$, and, hence, that $\sim(p \supset p)$ is true at $\langle \Omega, R, \varphi \rangle$. Since this is a contradiction, S cannot be satisfiable if inconsistent.

Base Case: $i = 1$. Suppose C_1 is an axiom or belongs to S. By Lemma 3 in the first case and by definition in the second, C_1 is true on $\langle \Omega, R, \varphi \rangle$.

Inductive Case: $i > 1$. Suppose for each $g < i$ that C_g is true on $\langle \Omega, R, \varphi \rangle$. Then if C_i is an axiom or a member of S, C_i is sure to be true on $\langle \Omega, R, \varphi \rangle$ by the argument above. So, suppose C_i follows from two previous entries, say

C_d and C_e $(= C_d \supset C_i)$, by RMP. Both are true on $\langle \Omega, R, \varphi \rangle$ by the hypothesis of the induction. So by the truth condition for $\supset$, C_i is true as well.

Hence for every i, C_i is true on $\langle \Omega, R, \varphi \rangle$ if S is satisfiable.

Thus, if S is inconsistent, S is *not* satisfiable.

Our Soundness Theorem is now at hand.

THEOREM 1. If $S \vdash A$ in K_t, then S entails A in K_t.

Proof: Suppose $S \vdash A$. Then $S \cup \{\sim A\}$ is inconsistent by Lemma 2(a). Hence, by Lemma 4, $S \cup \{\sim A\}$ is not satisfiable. Hence, by the definition of entailment, S entails A.

A special case of Theorem 1 is where $S = \emptyset$. Here, since $\vdash A$, A is sure to be a theorem, and by Theorem 1, $\emptyset$ entails A. Hence A is valid. (This is often called *Weak Soundness*.)

We now turn to the question of Completeness. The key lemma we have to establish is the converse of Lemma 4, i.e., if a set S is not satisfiable, then S is inconsistent. To do this we will show how to construct, given a consistent set S, a K_t-historical moment at which all the members of S are true. From this we can argue that if S is consistent in K_t, then S is K_t-satisfiable, and, hence, if S is not K_t-satisfiable, then S is not K_t-consistent. The crucial step in this construction consists in extending S to an infinitely large set S^∞ and showing that S^∞ is satisfiable in K_t.

Sundry definitions and lemmas are required before the actual construction can begin.

Any set S of statements is *maximally consistent* in K_t if it is both (i) consistent in K_t, and (ii) such that, for any statement A, if A is *not* a member of S, then $S \cup \{A\}$ is inconsistent in K_t.

Where S is a set of statements, the *Lindenbaum extension* S^∞ of S is as follows:[2]

(i) let S_0 be S; and

(ii) let S_n, for each n from 1 on, be $S_{n-1} \cup \{A_n\}$ — where A_n is the alphabetically n-th statement of K_t — if $S_{n-1} \cup \{A_n\}$ is consistent in K_t, and, if it isn't, let S_n be S_{n-1};

(iii) let S^∞ be the *union* of S_0, S_1, S_2, and so on.[3]

LEMMA 5. Where S^∞ is maximally consistent,

(a) For any statement A, if $S^\infty \vdash A$, then A belongs to S^∞

(b) For any negation $\sim A$, $\sim A$ belongs to S^∞ if and only if A doesn't

(c) For any conditional $A \supset B$, $A \supset B$ belongs to S^∞ if and only if either A does not belong or B does.

Proof: (a) Suppose $S^\infty \vdash A$ and, for a *reductio* further suppose that A is not a member of S^∞. Then $S \cup \{A\} \vdash \sim(p \supset p)$, and, hence, by A1 and Lemma 1(d), $S^\infty \vdash \sim A$. Hence, S^∞ is inconsistent, which defies the assumption on S^∞. Hence (a).

(b) By definition and Lemma 2(c), exactly one of A and $\sim A$ belongs to S^∞. Hence, (b).

(c) Suppose both $A \supset B$ and A belong to S^∞. Then, $S \vdash B$ by Lemma 1 (a) and (d). Hence, by (a) above, B belongs to S^∞. On the other hand, suppose A does not belong to S^∞, and, hence, that $\sim A$ does. Hence, by Lemma 1(a), $S^\infty \vdash \sim A$. By Lemma 1(a), $S^\infty \vdash \sim A \supset (\sim B \supset \sim A)$ (since $\sim A \supset (\sim B \supset \sim A)$ is an axiom by A1), hence, by Lemma 1(d), $S^\infty \vdash \sim B \supset \sim A$. But, by Lemma 1(a) and A1, again, $S^\infty \vdash (\sim B \supset \sim A) \supset (A \supset B)$, hence, $S^\infty \vdash A \supset B$, by Lemma 1(d), again. So, by (a), $A \supset B$ belongs to S^∞. Hence, (c).

LEMMA 6. Suppose S is K_t-consistent and S^∞ is the Lindenbaum extension of S. Then,

(a) For each n from 0 on, S_n is consistent in K_t,

(b) S^∞ is consistent, and

(c) S^∞ is maximally consistent.

Proof: (a) By the construction of S^∞, each S_n is sure to be consistent if S_{n-1} is. Proof by induction on n is left to the reader.

(b) Suppose S^∞ is inconsistent. Then, $S^\infty \vdash \sim(p \supset p)$, hence, by Lemma 1(b), $S_n \vdash \sim(p \supset p)$, for some n. But this is against the consistency of each S_n shown in (a). Hence, (b).

(c) Suppose A does not belong to S^∞, where A is the alphabetically n-th statement of K_t. Then A is sure not to belong to S_n, and, by the construction of S^∞, $S_n \cup \{A\}$ is inconsistent. Hence, by Lemma 1(c) and the definition of inconsistency, $S^\infty \cup \{A\}$ is inconsistent. Hence, (c).

LEMMA 7. Let S_B be a set of statements, S_{GB} be the result of prefacing every member of S_B by G, and S_{HB} the result of prefacing every member of S_B by H. Then,

(a) If $S_B \vdash A$, then $S_{GB} \vdash GA$, and

(b) If $S_B \vdash A$, then $S_{HB} \vdash HA$.

Proof: (a) Let $\{B_1, B_2, \ldots, B_k\}$ be a finite subset of S_B such that $\{B_1, B_2, \ldots, B_k\} \vdash A$ (that there is such a set is guarenteed by Lemma 1(b)). Then, by Lemma 1(e), $\vdash B_1 \supset (B_2 \supset (\ldots (B_k \supset A) \ldots))$. By $RG \supset$, $\vdash GB_1 \supset (GB_2 \supset (\ldots (GB_k \supset GA) \ldots))$. Hence, by Lemma 1(f), $\{GB_1, GB_2, \ldots, GB_k\} \vdash GA$. But, by hypothesis, GB_i $(1 \leqslant i \leqslant k)$ is a member of S_{GB} if B_i is a member of S_B. Hence, by Lemma 1(c), $S_{GB} \vdash GA$.

(b) Similar to (a), except with $RH \supset$ in place of $RG \supset$, etc.

Now for two more definitions. Suppose S^∞ is a maximally consistent set, $S_{[G]A}$ is the set consisting of every statement A such that GA belongs to S^∞, and $S_{[H]A}$ is the set consisting of every statement A such that HA belongs to S^∞. Then,

(i) Where FB is a member of S^∞, the Lindenbaum extension of $S_{[G]A} \cup \{B\}$ shall count as a *future attendant* of S^∞, and

(ii) Where PB' is a member of S^∞, the Lindebaum extension of $S_{[H]A} \cup \{B'\}$ shall count as a *past attendant* of S^∞.

It is crucial for our purposes that future and past attendants be maximally consistent. This immediately follows from the next Lemma and Lemma 6(c).

LEMMA 8. Let S^∞, $S_{[G]A}$, $S_{[H]A}$, FB, and PB' be as above. Then,

(a) $S_{[G]A} \cup \{B\}$ is consistent, and

(b) $S_{[H]A} \cup \{B'\}$ is consistent.

Proof: (a) Suppose, for a reductio ad absurdum, that $S_{[G]A} \cup \{B\}$ is inconsistent. Then $S_{[G]A} \cup \{B\} \vdash \sim(p \supset p)$, and, by Lemma 1(e), $S_{[G]A} \vdash B \supset \sim(p \supset p)$. By A1 (i.e., SC1 and SC22), Lemma 1(a), and Lemma 1(d), $S_{[G]A} \vdash \sim B$. Hence, by Lemma 7(a), $S_{GA} \vdash G \sim B$, where S_{GA} is the result of prefacing every member of $S_{[G]A}$ by G. But, S_{GA} is a subset of S^∞. Hence, by Lemma 1(b), $S^\infty \vdash G \sim B$. However, FB $(= \sim G \sim B)$ is a member of S^∞, hence, by Lemma 1(a), $S^\infty \vdash \sim G \sim B$, and, by Lemma 2(c), S^∞ is inconsistent. Hence, (a).

(b) Similar to (a), except with Lemma 7(b) in place of Lemma 7(a).

Finished with preliminary matters, we can now turn to the construction of $\langle \Omega, R, \varphi \rangle$ at which all the members of an arbitrary consistent set S are true.

Step 1

Take the set Ω_S to consist of (i) the Lindenbaum extension S^∞ of S, and (ii) the past and future attendants of every member of Ω_S (i.e., the past and future attendants of S^∞, their attendants, the attendants of their attendants, etc.). The members of Ω_S can be alphabetically ordered[4], so S^∞ will now be referred to as S_1^∞, and the other members of Ω_S are S_2^∞, S_3^∞, etc.

In view of Lemma 8 (and Lemma 6(c)), the members of Ω_S are sure to be maximally consistent.

Step 2

Define R_S, a dyadic relation on the members of Ω_S, as follows:

$R_S(S_i^\infty, S_j^\infty)$ if and only if – for any statement GA – A belongs to S_j^∞ if GA belongs to S_i^∞.

Two important features of R_S are recorded by the next lemma.

LEMMA 9. S_i^∞ and S_j^∞ are sets in Ω_S.

(a) If S_j^∞ is a future attendant of S_i^∞, or S_i^∞ is a past attendant of S_j^∞, then $R_S(S_i^\infty, S_j^\infty)$.

(b) $R_S(S_i^\infty, S_j^\infty)$ if and only if – for any statement HA – A belongs to S_i^∞ if HA belongs to S_j^∞.

Proof: (a) When S_j^∞ is a future attendant of S_i^∞, $R_S(S_i^\infty, S_j^\infty)$ by definition. So, suppose S_i^∞ is a past attendant of S_j^∞, and suppose A does not belong to S_j^∞. Then, by Lemma 5(b), $\sim A$ does belong to S_j^∞, and, hence, $S_j^\infty \vdash \sim A$ by Lemma 1(a). But $\sim A \supset HF \sim A$ is an axiom of K_t (A4), so by Lemma 1(a) and Lemma 1(d), $S_j^\infty \vdash HF \sim A$. Hence, by Lemma 5(a), $HF \sim A$ belongs to S_j^∞. Since S_i^∞ is a past attendant of S_j^∞, $F \sim A$ belongs to S_i^∞. Hence $\sim F \sim A$, by Lemma 5(b), does not belong to S_i^∞. So if GA ($= \sim F \sim A$) *does* belong to S_i^∞, then A belongs to S_j^∞. Hence, $R_S(S_i^\infty, S_j^\infty)$. Hence, (a).

(b) Suppose $R_S(S_i^\infty, S_j^\infty)$. Further suppose, for a *reductio*, for some statement HA, that HA belongs to S_j^∞ and A does *not* belong to S_i^∞. Then by Lemma 5(b), $\sim A$ belongs to S_i^∞. By A5, Lemma 5(a), and Lemma 1(a) and 1(b), then, $GP \sim A$ also belongs to S_i^∞. Hence, by the definition of R_S, $P \sim A$ belongs to S_j^∞. But $P \sim A$ is the same as $\sim HA$. Hence, by Lemma 1(a), both $S_j^\infty \vdash HA$ and $S_j^\infty \vdash \sim HA$, which contradicts the assumption on S_j^∞. On the other hand, suppose A belongs to S_i^∞ for every statement of the sort HA belonging to S_j^∞. Then, for a *reductio*, suppose it is not the case that $R_S(S_i^\infty, S_j^\infty)$. Then there is sure to be a statement of the sort GB in S_i^∞ such that $\sim B$ is a member of S_j^∞, by the definition of R_S and Lemma 1(b). By A4, Lemma 5(a), and Lemma 1(a) and 1(b), $HF \sim B$ is also a member of S_j^∞. Hence, from the assumption on S_i^∞ and S_j^∞, $F \sim B$ belongs to S_i^∞. But $F \sim B$ is the same as $\sim GB$. Hence, by Lemma 1(a), $S_i^\infty \vdash GB$ and $S_i^\infty \vdash \sim GB$, which contradicts the assumption on S_i^∞. Hence, (b).

Step 3

For each i from 1 on, take the *truth-value assignment corresponding to S_i^∞*

to be the result φ of assigning 1 to every statement letter in S_i^∞ and 0 to the remaining statement letters of K_t. Since the same truth-value assignment may correspond to several members of Ω_S, these assignments shall take the alphabetical ranks of the sets to which they correspond as their indices. (E.g., suppose φ corresponds to both S_i^∞ and S_j^∞. Then φ takes i as its index in the first case and j as its index in the second.)

Step 4

Take Ω to the the set of all of the (indexed) truth-value assignments which correspond to the members of Ω_S.

Step 5

Let R be the dyadic relation on the members of Ω such that — for any two members φ and μ of $\Omega - R(\varphi, \mu)$ if and only if $R_S(S_i^\infty, S_j^\infty)$, where φ corresponds to S_i^∞ and μ corresponds to S_j^∞.

To show that our construction of Ω and R does the trick, suppose φ is the truth-value assignment corresponding to S_1^∞, the Lindenbaum extension of our original set S. Then:

LEMMA 10. A statement A belongs to S_1^∞ if and only if A is true at $\langle \Omega, R, \varphi \rangle$.

Proof: By mathematical induction on the complexity of A, we show that A belongs to S_1^∞ if and only if A is true at $\langle \Omega, R, \varphi \rangle$.[6]

Base Case: A is a statement letter. By the definition of φ, A is sure to have value 1 if and only if A belongs to S_1^∞.

Inductive Case: Suppose for every statement A', less complex than A, that A' belongs to S_1^∞ if and only if A' is true at $\langle \Omega, R, \varphi \rangle$.

(i) Suppose, then, that A is either of the sort $\sim B$ or $B \supset C$. Then by the inductive hypothesis, Lemma 5(b) in the first case, Lemma 5(c) in the second case, and the truth conditions for $\sim$ and $\supset$, A is sure to belong to S_1^∞ if and only if A is true at $\langle \Omega, R, \varphi \rangle$.

(ii) Then take A to be of the sort FB. (a) Suppose there is no S_j^∞ in Ω_S such that $R_S(S_1^\infty, S_j^\infty)$, or no μ in Ω such that $R(\varphi, \mu)$. Then FB is sure not to belong to S_j^∞ and not to be true at $\langle \Omega, R, \varphi \rangle$. Hence, in this case, FB belongs to S_1^∞ if and only if FB is true at $\langle \Omega, R, \varphi \rangle$. (b) Suppose S_1^∞, has at least one future attendant. Then let FB belong to S_1^∞. Hence, in Ω_S, there is a set S_j^∞ such that both $R_S(S_1^\infty, S_j^\infty)$ and B belongs to S_j^∞. Then by the hypothesis of the induction, B is true at $\langle \Omega, R, \mu \rangle$, where μ corresponds to S_j^∞ and $R(\varphi, \mu)$. Then, FB is true at $\langle \Omega, R, \varphi \rangle$. On the other hand, suppose FB is true at $\langle \Omega, R, \varphi \rangle$. Then there is a μ in Ω such that $R(\varphi, \mu)$ and B is true at $\langle \Omega, R, \mu \rangle$.

Again by the hypothesis of the induction, B belongs to S_j^∞ and $R_S(S_1^\infty, S_j^\infty)$, where S_j^∞ is the set in Ω_S to which μ corresponds. By axiom A4 ($A \supset HFA$), Lemma 1(a), and Lemma 5(a), HFB consequently belongs to S_j^∞. Hence, by Lemma 9(b), FB belongs to S_1^∞. Hence, FB belongs to S_1^∞ if and only if FB is true at $\langle \Omega, R, \varphi \rangle$.

(iii) Suppose A is of the sort PB. Then by the same arguments as in (ii), except with axiom A5 ($A \supset GPA$) in place of A4 in part (b), PB belongs to S_1^∞ if and only if PB is true at $\langle \Omega, R, \varphi \rangle$. Thus, for any statement A, A belongs to S_1^∞ if and only if A is true at $\langle \Omega, R, \varphi \rangle$.

Lemma 10 shows that S_1^∞ is satisfiable in K_t, since all of its members are true on $\langle \Omega, R, \varphi \rangle$. But our original set S is a subset of S_1^∞. So it too is satisfiable in K_t. Generalizing on this result, we can hold that any consistent set is sure to be satisfiable, since the same construction as that above could be performed for it. Hence,

LEMMA 11. If S is consistent in K_t, then S is satisfiable in K_t.

Note, by contraposition, if S is not satisfiable in K_t, Lemma 11 assures us that it is inconsistent. This brings us to our Completeness Theorem.

THEOREM 2. If S entails A in K_t, then $S \vdash A$.

Proof: Suppose S entails A. Then $S \cup \{{\sim}A\}$ is not satisfiable, hence, by Lemma 11, $S \cup \{{\sim}A\}$ is inconsistent. Hence, by Lemma 2(b), $S \vdash A$.

A consequence of Theorem 2 is that when $S = \emptyset$ and A is a valid statement, $\vdash A$ and A is a theorem. This is often called *Weak Completeness*.

In the opening paragraph of this chapter, we promised to provide instructions for adapting the Soundness and Completeness Theorems for K_t to fit the other systems of tense logic. In the case of Soundness, it is only Lemma 3 which requires modification. Here an extra case is required for each axiom schema beyond those of K_t. These extra cases are similar to those given in Lemma 3 as it now stands — straightforward proofs of the validity of the axiom in question. As we have frequently pointed out, it is the additional properties required of the relation R through the systems which permit such proofs. So, with this single change, Theorem 1 will hold for any non-quantificational tense logic.

In the case of Theorem 2 — Completeness — an additional lemma is needed. We could safely assume prior to Lemma 10 that R as constructed was the appropriate relation for K_t-historical moments. This is due to the lack of any specified properties for R in the minimal system. In other systems, however, it must be shown that R has the appropriate properties and that the historical moment in which R occurs is indeed an historical moment of that system. The most natural strategy to produce this result is to follow Lemma 9 with the additional lemma and show, for each axiom beyond A7, that R_S has the property which corresponds to that axiom. Given our definition of R in Step 5, it will immediately follow that if R_S has a certain property, R has it as well.

Several illustrations of how such proofs would be run may make this point clearer. So,

(1) Suppose A11 ($GA \supset FA$) is an axiom in the system for which the construction is performed. We need to show that R_S (and, hence, R) will then have property P4, i.e., $(\forall x)(\exists y)R_S(x, y)$. This is tantamount to showing that every member of Ω_S has at least one future attendant. So, suppose there is a member S_i^∞ of Ω_S such that, for every member S_j^∞ of Ω_S, it is not the case that $R_S(S_i^\infty, S_j^\infty)$. Then, by the construction of Ω_S, $\sim\! FA$ belongs to S_i^∞ for every statement of the sort FA. Hence, for some B, both $\sim\! FB$ and $\sim\! F\!\sim\! B$ belong to S_i^∞. Hence, by Lemma 1(a), $S_i^\infty \vdash \sim\! F\!\sim\! B$ and $S_i^\infty \vdash \sim\! FB$. But, since $\sim\! F\!\sim\! B \supset FB$ is an axiom (A11, with $\sim\! F\!\sim$ for G), by Lemma 1(a), $S_i^\infty \vdash \sim\! F\!\sim\! B \supset FB$, and by Lemma 1(d), $S_i^\infty \vdash FB$. Hence, by Lemma 2(c), S_i^∞ is inconsistent, which defies the assumption on S_i^∞. So, if A11 is an axiom, then R_S, and, hence, R, has property P4.

(2) Suppose A8 ($FFA \supset FA$) is an axiom of the system. We need to show that R_S has property P1, i.e., $(\forall x)(\forall y)(\forall z)((R_S(x,y) \& R_S(y,z)) \supset R_S(x,z))$. Suppose, therefore, that for three sets in Ω_S S_i^∞, S_j^∞, and S_k^∞, both $R_S(S_i^\infty, S_j^\infty)$ and $R_S(S_j^\infty, S_k^\infty)$, but *not* $R_S(S_i^\infty, S_k^\infty)$. By the definition of R_S, then, there is a statement of the sort GA which belongs to S_i^∞, whereas A does not belong to S_k^∞. So, since $\sim\! A$ belongs to S_k^∞, so does $HF\!\sim\! A$ by A4, Lemma 1(a), and Lemma 5(a). Hence, by Lemma 9(b), $F\!\sim\! A$ belongs to S_j^∞. By the same argument, $HFF\!\sim\! A$ is sure to belong to S_j^∞, and, hence, $FF\!\sim\! A$ is sure to belong to S_i^∞. But, by Lemma 1(a), A8, and Lemma 1(d), $S_i^\infty \vdash GA$ and $S_i^\infty \vdash F\!\sim\! A$ ($= \sim\! GA$), as against the assumption on S_i^∞. Thus, $R_S(S_i^\infty, S_k^\infty)$, and R_S has property P1 if A8 is an axiom. Hence, R has P1 if A8 is an axiom.

(3) Suppose   A9 — ($FA \& FB) \supset (F(A \& B) \lor (F(A \& FB) \lor F(B \& FA)))$ — is an axiom. Then we need to demonstrate that R_S has property P2, i.e. $(\forall x)(\forall y)(\forall z)((R_S(x, y) \& R_S(x, z)) \supset ((y = z) \lor (R_S(y, z) \lor R_S(z, y))))$.

Suppose that S_i^∞, S_j^∞, and S_k^∞ are three sets in Ω_S such that $R_S(S_i^\infty, S_j^\infty)$ and $R_S(S_i^\infty, S_k^\infty)$. Further suppose that all of the following hold:

(a)   It is not the case that $R_S(S_j^\infty, S_k^\infty)$,

(b)   It is not the case that $R_S(S_k^\infty, S_j^\infty)$, and

(c) $S_j^\infty \neq S_k^\infty$.

Given the definition of R_S and (a), there is sure to be a statement of the sort GA in S_j^∞ such that A does not belong to S_k^∞. Given Lemma 9(b) and (b), there is sure to be a statement of the sort HB in S_j^∞ such that B does not belong to S_k^∞. And given (c) there is sure to be a statement C such that C *does not* belong to S_k^∞ and C *does* belong to S_j^∞. Hence, by Lemma 5(b), all of $\sim A$, $\sim B$, and $\sim C$ are members of S_k^∞. From SC26, RG⊃, and RH⊃, it is clear that each of the following statements is a theorem of K_t (and, hence, all of its enlargements):

$$GA \supset G{\sim}({\sim}A \,\&\, ({\sim}B \,\&\, {\sim}C))$$

$$HB \supset H{\sim}({\sim}A \,\&\, ({\sim}B \,\&\, {\sim}C))$$

$$C \supset {\sim}({\sim}A \,\&\, ({\sim}B \,\&\, {\sim}C))$$

Hence, by Lemma 1(c) and Lemma 5(a), each of the above is a member of S_j^∞. Since GA is a member of S_j^∞, by Lemma 5(c), $G{\sim}({\sim}A \,\&\, ({\sim}B \,\&\, {\sim}C))$ belongs to S_j^∞; since HB is a member of S_j^∞, $H{\sim}({\sim}A \,\&\, ({\sim}B \,\&\, {\sim}C))$ belongs to S_j^∞; and since C is a member of S_j^∞, ${\sim}({\sim}A \,\&\, ({\sim}B \,\&\, {\sim}C))$ also belongs to S_j^∞. From the proofs for T14 and T16, any enlargement of K_t with A9 among its axioms will have T17 $- (GA \,\&\, (A \,\&\, HA)) \supset HGA$ — as a theorem.
  Hence, by Lemma 1(c) and Lemma 5(a),

$$(G{\sim}({\sim}A \,\&\, ({\sim}B \,\&\, {\sim}C)) \,\&\, ({\sim}({\sim}A \,\&\, ({\sim}B \,\&\, {\sim}C))$$
$$\&\, H{\sim}({\sim}A \,\&\, ({\sim}B \,\&\, {\sim}C)))) \supset HG{\sim}({\sim}A \,\&\, ({\sim}B \,\&\, {\sim}C))$$

is a member of S_j^∞. Hence, by Lemma 1(c),

$$HG{\sim}({\sim}A \,\&\, ({\sim}B \,\&\, {\sim}C))$$

is a member of S_j^∞. Therefore, $G{\sim}({\sim}A \,\&\, ({\sim}B \,\&\, {\sim}C))$ is a member of S_i^∞ by Lemma 9(b) and the hypothesis on R_S. Hence, by the definition of R_S and the assumption that $R_S(S_i^\infty, S_k^\infty)$, ${\sim}({\sim}A \,\&\, ({\sim}B \,\&\, {\sim}C)$ is a member of S_k^∞. Hence, by Lemma 1(a), $S_k^\infty \vdash {\sim}({\sim}A \,\&\, ({\sim}B \,\&\, {\sim}C))$. But $\sim A$, $\sim B$, and $\sim C$ belong to S_k^∞. Hence. by Lemma 1(a), again, $S \vdash {\sim}A \,\&\, ({\sim}B \,\&\, {\sim}C)$, which contradicts the assumption on S_k^∞. Hence, one of (a)–(c) must be false, hence, R_S has property P2. Hence, R has property P2 if A9 is an axiom.

With this extra lemma in hand, Lemma 10 is certain to show that S_1^∞ is satisfiable within the appropriate system, and, hence, that any consistent set of that system is satisfiable as well. This leads to Theorem 2 by the same argument as was given in the case of K_t.

The above remarks apply to the general non-quantificational case, with the single exception of OT. Here, in addition to additions to Lemma 3 for each of the ten axioms beyond those of K_t, some changes are required to the construction in order to secure Lemma 10. These are necessitated by the two relations in the OT-historical moments. Furthermore, for each of the three quantificational bases, several additional lemmas are required for the Soundness Theorem, and much of the construction and the prefatory material requires revision. The additional material needed by the Q systems, although tedious, is easily adapted from the literature on Henkin-style completeness proofs for standard quantificational logics. The $Q*$ and $Q**$ systems, on the other hand, need even more. Portions of the overall strategy behind the construction have to be altered, in order to see through the proof of Lemma 10.[6]

NOTES

[1] The general outlines of our Soundness and Completeness proofs are due to Makinson, 1966 and Leblanc, 1976.

[2] It is a routine matter, familiar from standard treatments of classical logic, to arrange the statements of a system in a definite order. So we feel free to speak here of the alphabetical place of a statement in such an ordering, and presume the statements of K_t to have been so ordered. We shall also assume that this ordering is based on the complexity of a statement, so, e.g., A preceeds $\sim A$, A and B preceed $A \supset B$, and A preceeds FB and PB.

[3] S^∞ is certain to be of cardinality aleph$_0$, hence the appropriateness of the superscript.

[4] This ordering of the members of Ω_S – and assigning them indices based upon it – is necessitated by the fact that two such sets may have identical memberships. The ordering, found in McArthur, 1972, Appendix I, assigns to each set a positive integer. An upshot of this procedure is the denumerability of Ω_S no matter what the initial set S. Hence Ω in the constructed historical moment $\langle \Omega, R, \varphi \rangle$ is sure to be denumerable (at most), and thus a Lowenheim-Skolem Theorem is available for K_t insofar as this shows it to have a denumerable model.

[5] Since we presume the statements of K_t to have an alphabetical order based on complexity (see note 2) we can run this induction on the complexity of A.

[6] See McArthur and Leblanc, 1975.

SC TAUTOLOGIES USED IN PROOFS

SC1. $(A \supset B) \supset (\sim B \supset \sim A)$

SC2. $(A \supset B) \supset ((B \supset C) \supset (A \supset C))$

SC3. $A \supset (A \lor B)$

SC4. $B \supset (A \lor B)$

SC5. $(A \supset C) \supset ((B \supset C) \supset ((A \lor B) \supset C))$

SC6. $\sim(\sim A \lor \sim B) \equiv (A \mathbin{\&} B)$

SC7. $(A \mathbin{\&} B) \supset A$

SC8. $(A \mathbin{\&} B) \supset B$

SC9. $(A \supset B) \supset ((A \supset C) \supset (A \supset (B \mathbin{\&} C)))$

SC10. $A \supset (B \supset (A \mathbin{\&} B))$

SC11. $(A \supset (B \supset C)) \supset ((A \mathbin{\&} B) \supset C)$

SC12. $(A \supset B) \supset ((B \supset A) \supset (A \equiv B))$

SC13. $\sim(\sim A \mathbin{\&} \sim B) \equiv (A \lor B)$

SC14. $(\sim A \equiv \sim B) \supset (A \equiv B)$

SC15. $A \equiv \sim\sim A$

SC16. $\sim(\sim A \mathbin{\&} (B \mathbin{\&} (A \mathbin{\&} C)))$

SC17. $(A \mathbin{\&} B) \equiv (B \mathbin{\&} A)$

SC18. $(\sim A \supset \sim B) \equiv \sim(\sim A \mathbin{\&} B)$

SC19. $(A \lor B) \equiv (B \lor A)$

SC20. $\sim B \supset ((A \supset B) \supset \sim A)$

SC21. $\sim(A \mathbin{\&} B) \equiv (A \supset B)$

SC22. $A \supset A$

SC23. $(A \supset B) \supset ((A \mathbin{\&} C) \supset B)$

SC24. $(A \lor B) \supset ((B \supset A) \supset A)$

SC25. $(A \supset (B \supset C)) \supset (B \supset (A \supset C))$

SC26. $A \supset \sim(\sim A \mathbin{\&} (\sim B \mathbin{\&} \sim C))$

SUMMARY OF THE SYSTEMS

1 AXIOMS

A1. A, where A is a tautology

A2. $G(A \supset B) \supset (GA \supset GB)$

A3. $H(A \supset B) \supset (HA \supset HB)$

A4. $A \supset HFA$

A5. $A \supset GPA$

A6. GA, where A is an axiom

A7. HA, where A is an axiom

A8. $FFA \supset FA$

A9. $(FA \& FB) \supset (F(A \& B) \vee ((F(A \& FB) \vee F(FA \& B)))$

A10. $(PA \& PB) \supset (P(A \& B) \vee ((P(A \& PB) \vee P(PA \& B)))$

A11. $GA \supset FA$

A12. $HA \supset PA$

A13. $FA \supset FFA$

A14. $GA \supset A$

A15. $GA \supset HA$

A16. $L(A \supset B) \supset (LA \supset LB)$

A17. $MMA \supset MA$

A18. LA, where A is an axiom

A19. $LA \supset GA$ T37. $G(\forall X)A \supset (\forall X)GA$

A20. $A \supset LPA$ T38. $H(\forall X)A \supset (\forall X)HA$

M1. $LA \supset A$

M2. same as A16

M3. same as A18

M4. same as A17

M5. $(L(A \vee B) \& (L(A \vee LB) \& L(LA \vee B))) \supset (LA \vee LB)$

M6. $MLA \supset A$

M7. $MLA \supset LA$

Q1. $(\forall X)(A \supset B) \supset ((\forall X)A \supset (\forall X)B)$

Q2. $A \supset (\forall X)A$

Q3. $(\forall X)A \supset A(C/X)$

Q3*a. $(\forall X)((\forall Y)A \supset A(Y/X))$

Q3*b. $(\forall X)(\forall Y)A \supset (\forall Y)(\forall X)A$

Q4. $(\forall X)A$, where, for some individual constant C foreign to $(\forall X)A$, $A(C/X)$ is an axiom

Q5. $(\forall X)A \supset A(C/X)$, where A contains no tense operators

2. TENSE LOGICS (All systems have RMP as a rule of inference)

K_t (Lemmon)
A1−A7

CR (Cocchiarella)
A1−A8

K_b (Rescher and Urquhart)
A1−A8, A10

CL (Cocchiarella)
A1−A10

SL (Scott)
A1−A12

PL (Prior)
A1−A13

PCr (Prior)
A1−A8, A14−A15

OT
A1−A12, A16−A20

QK_t
Q1−Q4, A2−A7

QK_t^*
Q1−Q2, Q3*a−Q3*b, Q4, A2−A7

QK_t^{**}
Q1−Q2, Q3*a−Q3*b, Q4−Q5, A2−A7, T37−T38

3. MODAL LOGICS (All have RMP)

M
A1, M1—M3

S_4
A1, M1—M4

$S_{4.3}$
A1, M1—M5

B
A1, M1—M3, M6

S_5
A1, M1—M4, M7

BIBLIOGRAPHY

Cocchiarella, Nino B.: 1966, *Tense Logic: A Study in the Topology of Time*, (Ph.D. Thesis, University of California at Los Angeles, 1966).

Hintikka, K. J. J.: 1959, 'Existential Presuppositions and Existential Committments', *Journal of Philosophy*, vol. 56 (1959), pp. 125–137.

Hintikka, K. J. J.: 1969, *Models for Modalities*, (New York: Humanities Press, 1969).

Hughes, J. E. and Cresswell, M. J.: 1968, *Modal Logic* (New York: Barnes and Noble, 1968).

Kripke, Saul A.: 1963, 'Semantical Considerations on Modal Logic', *Acta Philosophica Fennica*, Fasc. **XVI** (1963), pp. 83–94.

Kamp, Hans: 1971, 'Formal Properties of 'Now'', *Theoria* 37 (1971), pp. 227–273.

Leblanc, Hugues: 1972, 'On Dispensing With Things and Worlds', in *Existence and Possible Worlds* (New York: New York University Press, 1972).

Leblanc, H.: 1976, *Truth-Value Semantics* (Amsterdam: North-Holland Publishing Co., 1976).

Leblanc, Hugues and Hailperin, Theodore: 1959, 'Nondesignating Singular Terms',

Mates, Benson: 1952, *Stoic Logic* (Los Angeles: University of California Press, 1952).

Makinson, David: 1966, 'On Some Completeness Theorems in Modal Logic', *Zeitschrift fur Mathematische Logik und Grundlagen der Mathematik*, Band **12** (1966), pp. 379–384.

McArthur, Robert P.: 1972, *Truth-Value Semantics for Tense Logics* (Ph.D. Thesis, Temple University, 1972).

McArthur, R. P.: 1975, 'Ockham's Tense Logic', forthcoming.

McArthur, Robert P. and Leblanc, Hugues: 1975, 'A Completeness Result for Quantificational Tense Logic', *Zeitschrift fur Mathematische Logik und Grundlagen der Mathematik*, forthcoming.

Prior, A. N.: 1966, 'Postulates for Tense Logic', *American Philosophical Quarterly* (April, 1966), pp. 153–161.

Prior, A. N.: 1967, *Past, Present, and Future* (Oxford: Oxford University Press, 1967).

Quine, W. V. O.: 1953, 'Mr. Strawson on Logical Theory', *Mind*, vol. **63** (1953), pp. 433–451.

Quine, W. V. O.: 1960, *Word and Object* (Cambridge, Mass.: Massachusetts Institute of Technology Press, 1960).

Rennie, M. K.: 1969, 'Postulates for Temporal Order', *The Monist*, (vol. 53) (1969), pp. 457–468.

Rescher, Nicholas: 1969, *Many Valued Logic* (New York: McGraw Hill, Inc., 1969).

Rescher, Nicholas and Urquhart, Alasdair: 1971, *Temporal Logic* (New York: Springer-Verlag, 1971).

Strawson, P. F.: 1952, *Introduction to Logical Theory* (New York: Barnes and Noble, 1952).

Thomason, Richmond: 1970a, 'Indeterministic Time and Truth-value Gaps', *Theoria*, vol. 36 (1970), pp. 264–281.

Thomason, Richmond: 1970b, *Symbolic Logic: An Introduction* (New York: The Macmillan Co., 1970).

Wittgenstein, Ludwig: 1961, *Tractatus Logico-Philosophicus* (London: Routledge & Kegan Paul, 1961).

SYNTHESE LIBRARY

Monographs on Epistemology, Logic, Methodology,
Philosophy of Science, Sociology of Science and of Knowledge, and on the
Mathematical Methods of Social and Behavioral Sciences

Managing Editor:

JAAKKO HINTIKKA (Academy of Finland and Stanford University)

Editors:

ROBERT S. COHEN (Boston University)
DONALD DAVIDSON (The Rockefeller University and Princeton University)
GABRIËL NUCHELMANS (University of Leyden)
WESLEY C. SALMON (University of Arizona)

1. J. M. BOCHEŃSKI, *A Precis of Mathematical Logic.* 1959, X + 100 pp.
2. P. L. GUIRAUD, *Problèmes et méthodes de la statistique linguistique.* 1960, VI + 146 pp.
3. HANS FREUDENTHAL (ed.), *The Concept and the Role of the Model in Mathematics and Natural and Social Sciences, Proceedings of a Colloquium held at Utrecht, The Netherlands, January 1960.* 1961, VI + 194 pp.
4. EVERT W. BETH, *Formal Methods. An Introduction to Symbolic Logic and the Study of effective Operations in Arithmetic and Logic.* 1962, XIV + 170 pp.
5. B. H. KAZEMIER and D. VUYSJE (eds.), *Logic and Language. Studies dedicated to Professor Rudolf Carnap on the Occasion of his Seventieth Birthday.* 1962, VI + 256 pp.
6. MARX W. WARTOFSKY (ed.), *Proceedings of the Boston Colloquium for the Philosophy of Science, 1961–1962*, Boston Studies in the Philosophy of Science (ed. by Robert S. Cohen and Marx W. Wartofsky), Volume I. 1973, VIII + 212 pp.
7. A. A. ZINOV'EV, *Philosophical Problems of Many-Valued Logic.* 1963. XIV + 155 pp.
8. GEORGES GURVITCH, *The Spectrum of Social Time.* 1964, XXVI + 152 pp.
9. PAUL LORENZEN, *Formal Logic.* 1965, VIII + 123 pp.
10. ROBERT S. COHEN and MARX W. WARTOFSKY (eds.), *In Honor of Philipp Frank*, Boston Studies in het Philosophy of Science (ed. by Robert S. Cohen and Marx W. Wartofsky), Volume II. 1965, XXXIV + 475 pp.
11. EVERT W. BETH, *Mathematical Thought. An Introduction to the Philosopy of Mathematics.* 1965, XII + 208 pp.
12. EVERT W. BETH and JEAN PIAGET, *Mathematical Epistemology and Psychology.* 1966, XII + 326 pp.
13. GUIDO KÜNG, *Ontology and the Logistic Analysis of Language. An Enquiry into the Contemporary Views on Universals.* 1967, XI + 210 pp.
14. ROBERT S. COHEN and MARX W. WARTOFSKY (eds.), *Proceedings of the Boston Colloquium for the Philosophy of Science 1964–1966, in Memory of Norwood Russell Hanson*, Boston Studies in the Philosophy of Science (ed. by Robert S. Cohen and Marx W. Wartofsky), Volume III. 1967, XLIX + 489 pp.

15. C. D. BROAD, *Induction, Probability, and Causation. Selected Papers*. 1968, XI + 296 pp.
16. GÜNTHER PATZIG, *Aristotle's Theory of the Syllogism. A logical-Philosophical Study of Book A of the Prior Analytics*. 1968, XVII + 215 pp.
17. NICHOLAS RESCHER, *Topics in Philosophical Logic*. 1968, XIV + 347 pp.
18. ROBERT S. COHEN and MARX W. WARTOFSKY (eds.), *Proceedings of the Boston Colloquium for the Philosophy of Science 1966–1968*, Boston Studies in the Philosophy of Science (ed. by Robert S. Cohen and Marx W. Wartofsky), Volume IV. 1969, VIII + 537 pp.
19. ROBERT S. COHEN and MARX W. WARTOFSKY (eds.), *Proceedings of the Boston Colloquium for the Philosophy of Science 1966–1968*, Boston Studies in the Philosophy of Science (ed. by Robert S. Cohen and Marx W. Wartofsky), Volume V. 1969, VIII + 482 pp.
20. J. W. DAVIS, D. J. HOCKNEY, and W. K. WILSON (eds.), *Philosophical Logic*. 1969, VIII + 277 pp.
21. D. DAVIDSON and J. HINTIKKA (eds.), *Words and Objections. Essays on the Work of W. V. Quine*. 1969, VIII + 366 pp.
22. PATRICK SUPPES, *Studies in the Methodology and Foundations of Science. Selected Papers from 1911 to 1969*, XII + 473 pp.
23. JAAKKO HINTIKKA, *Models for Modalities. Selected Essays*. 1969, IX + 220 pp.
24. NICHOLAS RESCHER et al. (eds.), *Essays in Honor of Carl G. Hempel. A Tribute on the Occasion of his Sixty-Fifth Birthday*. 1969, VII + 272 pp.
25. P.V. TAVANEC (ed.), *Problems of the Logic of Scientific Knowledge*. 1969, VII + 429 pp.
26. MARSHALL SWAIN (ed.), *Induction, Acceptance, and Rational Belief*. 1970, VII + 232 pp.
27. ROBERT S. COHEN and RAYMOND J. SEEGER (eds.), *Ernst Mach: Physicist and Philosopher*, Boston Studies in the Philosophy of Science (ed. by Robert S. Cohen and Marx W. Wartofsky), Volume VI. 1970, VIII + 295 pp.
28. JAAKKO HINTIKKA and PATRICK SUPPES, *Information and Inference*. 1970, X + 336 pp.
29. KAREL LAMBERT, *Philosophical Problems in Logic. Some Recent Developments*. 1970, VII + 176 pp.
30. ROLF A. EBERLE, *Nominalistic Systems*. 1970, IX + 217 pp.
31. PAUL WEINGARTNER and GERHARD ZECHA (eds.), *Induction, Physics, and Ethics. Proceedings and Discussions of the 1968 Salzburg Colloquium in the Philosophy of Science*. 1970, X + 382 pp.
32. EVERT W. BETH, *Aspects of Modern Logic*. 1970, XI + 176 pp.
33. RISTO HILPINEN (ed.), *Deontic Logic: Introductory and Systematic Readings*. 1971, VII + 182 pp.
34. JEAN-LOUIS KRIVINE, *Introduction to Axiomatic Set Theory*. 1971, VII + 98 pp.
35. JOSEPH D. SNEED, *The Logical Structure of Mathematical Physics*. 1971, XV + 311 pp.
36. CARL R. KORDIG, *The Justification of Scientific Change*. 1971, XIV + 119 pp.
37. MILIČ ČAPEK, *Bergson and Modern Physics*, Boston Studies in the Philosophy of Science (ed. by Robert S. Cohen and Marx W. Wartofsky), Volume VII. 1971, XV + 414 pp.
38. NORWOOD RUSSELL HANSON, *What I do Not Believe, and Other Essays* (ed. by Stephen Toulmin and Harry Woolf), 1971, XII + 390 pp.
39. ROGER C. BUCK and ROBERT S. COHEN (eds.), *PSA 1970. In Memory of Rudolf Carnap*, Boston Studies in the Philosophy of Science (ed. by Robert S. Cohen and Marx W. Wartofsky), Volume VIII. 1971, LXVI + 615 pp. Also available as paperback.
40. DONALD DAVIDSON and GILBERT HARMAN (eds.), *Semantics of Natural Language*. 1972, X + 769 pp. Also available as paperback.

41. YEHOSHUA BAR-HILLEL (ed.), *Pragmatics of Natural Languages.* 1971, VII + 231 pp.
42. SÖREN STENLUND, *Combinators, λ-Terms and Proof Theory.* 1972, 184 pp.
43. MARTIN STRAUSS, *Modern Physics and Its Philosophy. Selected Papers in the Logic, History, and Philosophy of Science.* 1972, X + 297 pp.
44. MARIO BUNGE, *Method, Model and Matter.* 1973, VII + 196 pp.
45. MARIO BUNGE, *Philosophy of Physics.* 1973, IX + 248 pp.
46. A. A. ZINOV'EV, *Foundations of the Logical Theory of Scientific Knowledge (Complex Logic),* Boston Studies in the Philosophy of Science (ed. by Robert S. Cohen and Marx W. Wartofsky), Volume IX. Revised and enlarged English edition with an appendix, by G. A. Smirnov, E. A. Sidorenka, A. M. Fedina, and L. A. Bobrova. 1973, XXII + 301 pp. Also available as paperback.
47. LADISLAV TONDL, *Scientific Procedures,* Boston Studies in the Philosophy of Science (ed. by Robert S. Cohen and Marx W. Wartofsky), Volume X. 1973, XII + 268 pp. Also available as paperback.
48. NORWOOD RUSSELL HANSON, *Constellations and Conjectures,* (ed. by Willard C. Humphreys, Jr.), 1973, X + 282 pp.
49. K. J. J. HINTIKKA, J. M. E. MORAVCSIK, and P. SUPPES (eds.), *Approaches to Natural Language. Proceedings of the 1970 Stanford Workshop on Grammar and Semantics.* 1973, VIII + 526 pp. Also available as paperback.
50. MARIO BUNGE (ed.), *Exact Philosophy – Problems, Tools, and Goals.* 1973, X + 214 pp.
51. RADU J. BOGDAN and ILKKA NIINILUOTO (eds.), *Logic, Language, and Probability.* A selection of papers contributed to Sections IV, VI, and XI of the Fourth International Congress for Logic, Methodology, and Philosophy of Science, Bucharest, September 1971. 1973, X + 323 pp.
52. GLENN PEARCE and PATRICK MAYNARD (eds.), *Conceptual Chance.* 1973, XII + 282 pp.
53. ILKKA NIINILUOTO and RAIMO TUOMELA, *Theoretical Concepts and Hypothetico-Inductive Inference.* 1973, VII + 264 pp.
54. ROLAND FRAÏSSÉ, *Course of Mathematical Logic – Volume 1: Relation and Logical Formula.* 1973, XVI + 186 pp. Also available as paperback.
55. ADOLF GRÜNBAUM, *Philosophical Problems of Space and Time.* Second, enlarged edition, Boston Studies in the Philosophy of Science (ed. by Robert S. Cohen and Marx W. Wartofsky), Volume XII. 1973, XXIII + 884 pp. Also available as paperback.
56. PATRICK SUPPES (ed.), *Space, Time, and Geometry.* 1973, XI + 424 pp.
57. HANS KELSEN, *Essays in Legal and Moral Philosophy,* selected and introduced by Ota Weinberger. 1973, XXVIII + 300 pp.
58. R. J. SEEGER and ROBERT S. COHEN (eds.), *Philosophical Foundations of Science. Proceedings of an AAAS Program, 1969.* Boston Studies in the Philosophy of Science (ed. by Robert S. Cohen and Marx W. Wartofsky), Volume XI. 1974, X + 545 pp. Also available as paperback.
59. ROBERT S. COHEN and MARX W. WARTOFSKY (eds.), *Logical and Epistemological Studies in Contemporary Physics,* Boston Studies in the Philosophy of Science (ed. by Robert S. Cohen and Marx W. Wartofsky), Volume XIII. 1973, VIII + 462 pp. Also available as paperback.
60. ROBERT S. COHEN and MARX W. WARTOFSKY (eds.), *Methodological and Historical Essays in the Natural and Social Sciences. Proceedings of the Boston Colloquium for the Philosophy of Science, 1969–1972,* Boston Studies in the Philosophy of Science (ed. by Robert S. Cohen and Marx W. Wartofsky), Volume XIV. 1974, VIII + 405 pp. Also available as paperback.
61. ROBERT S. COHEN, J. J. STACHEL and MARX W. WARTOFSKY (eds.), *For Dirk Struik.*

Scientific, Historical and Polical Essays in Honor of Dirk J. Struik, Boston Studies in the Philosophy of Science (ed. by Robert S. Cohen and Marx W. Wartofsky), Volume XV. 1974, XXVII + 652 pp. Also available as paperback.

62. KAZIMIERZ AJDUKIEWICZ, *Pragmatic Logic*, transl. from the Polish by Olgierd Wojtasiewicz. (1974, XV + 460 pp.

63. SÖREN STENLUND (ed.), *Logical Theory and Semantic Analysis. Essays Dedicated to Stig Kanger on His Fiftieth Birthday*. 1974, V + 217 pp.

64. KENNETH F. SCHAFFNER and ROBERT S. COHEN (eds.), *Proceedings of the 1972 Biennial Meeting, Philosophy of Science Association*, Boston Studies in the Philosophy of Science (ed. by Robert S. Cohen and Marx W. Wartofsky), Volume XX. 1974, IX + 444 pp. Also available as paperback.

65. HENRY E. KYBURG, JR., *The Logical Foundations of Statistical Inference*. 1974, IX + 421 pp.

66. MARJORIE GRENE, *The Understanding of Nature: Essays in the Philosophy of Biology*, Boston Studies in the Philosophy of Science (ed. by Robert S. Cohen and Marx W. Wartofsky), Volume XXIII. 1974, XII + 360 pp. Also available as paperback.

67. JAN M. BROEKMAN, *Stucturalism: Moscow, Prague, Paris*. 1974, IX + 117 pp.

68. NORMAN GESCHWIND, *Selected Papers on Language and the Brain*, Boston Studies in the Philosophy of Science (ed. by Robert S. Cohen and Marx W. Wartofsky), Volume XVI. 1974, XII + 549 pp. Also available as paperback.

69. ROLAND FRAÏSSÉ, *Course of Mathematical Logic* – Volume II: *Model Theory*. 1974, XIX + 192 pp.

70. ANDRZEJ GRZEGORCZYK, *An Outline of Methematical Logic. Fundamental Results and Notions Explained with All Details*. 1974, X + 596 pp.

71. FRANZ VON KUTSCHERA, *Philosophy of Language*. 1975, VII + 305 pp.

72. JUHA MANNINEN and RAIMO TUOMELA (eds.), *Essays on Explanation and Understanding. Studies in the Foundations of Humanities and Social Sciences*. 1976, VII + 440 pp.

73. JAAKKO HINTIKKA (ed.), *Rudolf Carnap, Logical Empiricist. Materials and Perspectives*. 1975, LXVIII + 400 pp.

74. MILIČ ČAPEK (ed.), *The Concepts of Space and Time. Their Structure and Their Development*. Boston Studies in the Philosophy of Science (ed. by Robert S. Cohen and Marx W. Wartofsky), Volume XXII. 1976, LVI + 570 pp. Also available as paperback.

75. JAAKKO HINTIKKA and UNTO REMES, *The Method of Analysis. Its Geometrical Origin and Its General Significance*. Boston Studies in the Philosophy of Science (ed. by Robert S. Cohen and Marx W. Wartofsky), Volume XXV. 1974, XVIII + 144 pp. Also available as paperback.

76. JOHN EMERY MURDOCH and EDITH DUDLEY SYLLA, *The Cultural Context of Medieval Learning. Proceedings of the First International Colloquium on Philosophy, Science, and Theology in the Middle Ages – September 1973*. Boston Studies in the Philosophy of Science (ed. by Robert S. Cohen and Marx W. Wartofsky), Volume XXVI. 1975, X + 566 pp. Also available as paperback.

77. STEFAN AMSTERDAMSKI, *Between Experience and Metaphysics. Philosophical Problems of the Evolution of Science*. Boston Studies in the Philosophy of Science (ed. by Robert S. Cohen and Marx W. Wartofsky), Volume XXXV. 1975, XVIII + 193 pp. Also available as paperback.

78. PATRICK SUPPES (ed.), *Logic and Probability in Quantum Mechanics*. 1976, XV + 541 pp.

80. JOSEPH AGASSI, *Science in Flux*. Boston Studies in the Philosophy of Science (ed. by Robert S. Cohen and Marx W. Wartofsky), Volume XXVIII. 1975, XXVI + 553 pp. Also available as paperback.

81. SANDRA G. HARDING (ed.), *Can Theories Be Refuted? Essays on the Duhem-Quine Thesis.* 1976, XXI + 318 pp. Also available as paperback.

84. MARJORIE GRENE and EVERETT MENDELSOHN (eds.), *Topics in the Philosophy of Biology.* Boston Studies in the Philosophy of Science (ed. by Robert S. Cohen and Marx W. Wartofsky), Volume XXVII. 1976, XIII + 454 pp. Also available as paperback.

85. E. FISCHBEIN, *The Intuitive Sources of Probabilistic Thinking in Children.* 1975, XIII + 204 pp.

86. ERNEST W. ADAMS, *The Logic of Conditionals. An Application of Probability to Deductive Logic.* 1975, XIII + 156 pp.

89. A. KASHER (ed.), *Language in Focus: Foundations, Methods and Systems. Essays Dedicated to Yehoshua Bar-Hillel.* Boston Studies in the Philosophy of Science (ed. by Robert S. Cohen and Marx W. Wartofsky), Volume XLIII. 1976, XXVIII + 679 pp. Also available as paperback.

90. JAAKKO HINTIKKA, *The Intentions of Intentionality and Other New Models for Modalities.* 1975, XVIII + 262 pp. Also available as paperback.

93. RADU J. BOGDAN, *Local Induction.* 1976, XIV + 340 pp.

95. PETER MITTELSTAEDT, *Philosophical Problems of Modern Physics.* Boston Studies in the Philosophy of Science (ed. by Robert S. Cohen and Marx W. Wartofsky), Volume XVIII. 1976, X + 211 pp. Also available as paperback.

96. GERALD HOLTON and WILLIAM BLANPIED (eds.), *Science and Its Public: The Changing Relationship.* Boston Studies in the Philosophy of Science (ed. by Robert S. Cohen and Marx W. Wartofsky), Volume XXXIII. 1976, XXV + 289 pp. Also available as paperback.

SYNTHESE HISTORICAL LIBRARY

Texts and Studies
in the History of Logic and Philosophy

Editors:

N. KRETZMANN (Cornell University)
G. NUCHELMANS (University of Leyden)
L. M. DE RIJK (University of Leyden)

1. M. T. BEONIO-BROCCHIERI FUMAGALLI, *The Logic of Abelard*. Translated from the Italian. 1969, IX + 101 pp.
2. GOTTFRIED WILHELM LEIBNITZ, *Philosophical Papers and Letters*. A selection translated and edited, with an introduction, by Leroy E. Loemker. 1969, XII + 736 pp.
3. ERNST MALLY, *Logische Schriften*, ed. by Karl Wolf and Paul Weingartner. 1971, X + 340 pp.
4. LEWIS WHITE BECK (ed.), *Proceedings of the Third International Kant Congress*. 1972, XI + 718 pp.
5. BERNARD BOLZANO, *Theory of Science*, ed. by Jan Berg. 1973, XV + 398 pp.
6. J. M. E. MORAVCSIK (ed.), *Patterns in Plato's Thought. Papers arising out of the 1971 West Coast Greek Philosophy Conference*. 1973, VIII + 212 pp.
7. NABIL SHEHABY, *The Propositional Logic of Avicenna: A Translation from al-Shifā: al-Qiyās*, with Introduction, Commentary and Glossary. 1973, XIII + 296 pp.
8. DESMOND PAUL HENRY, *Commentary on De Grammatico: The Historical-Logical Dimensions of a Dialogue of St. Anselm's*. 1974, IX + 345 pp.
9. JOHN CORCORAN, *Ancient Logic and Its Modern Interpretations*. 1974, X + 208 pp.
10. E. M. BARTH, *The Logic of the Articles in Traditional Philosophy*. 1974, XXVII + 533 pp.
11. JAAKKO HINTIKKA, *Knowledge and the Known. Historical Perspectives in Epistemology*. 1974, XII + 243 pp.
12. E. J. ASHWORTH, *Language and Logic in the Post-Medieval Period*. 1974, XIII + 304 pp.
13. ARISTOTLE, *The Nicomachean Ethics*. Translated with Commentaries and Glossary by Hypocrates G. Apostle. 1975, XXI + 372 pp.
14. R. M. DANCY, *Sense and Contradiction: A Study in Aristotle*. 1975, XII + 184 pp.
15. WILBUR RICHARD KNORR, *The Evolution of the Euclidean Elements. A Study of the Theory of Incommensurable Magnitudes and Its Significance for Early Greek Geometry*. 1975, IX + 374 pp.
16. AUGUSTINE, *De Dialectica*. Translated with the Introduction and Notes by B. Darrell Jackson. 1975, XI + 151 pp.